Introduction to Writing Goals and Objectives:

A Manual for Recreation Therapy Students and Entry-Level Professionals

by

Suzanne Melcher, TRS/CTRS

Introduction to Writing Goals and Objectives:

A Manual for Recreation Therapy Students and Entry-Level Professionals

by

Suzanne Melcher, TRS/CTRS

Venture Publishing, Inc.

1999 Cato Avenue, State College, PA 16801

Venture Publishing, Inc.
1999 Cato Avenue
State College, PA 16801
Phone (814) 234–4561; Fax (814) 234–1651

Excerpts from Mager, Robert F. (1984) *Preparing Instructional Objectives* reprinted with permission. Published by The Center for Effective Performance, 2300 Peachford Road, Suite 2000, Atlanta, GA 30338. 1-800-558-4237.

Production Manager: Richard Yocum
Manuscript Editing: Michele L. Barbin and Deborah L. McRann
Cover Design and Typesetting: Michele L. Barbin

ISBN 1-892132-10-9

This workbook is dedicated to my mentor, Pam Wilson, M.S., TRS/CTRS.

It is my hope that I will one day be as fine a teacher as she.

Contents

Acknowledgments

Much appreciation goes to Leandra Bedini, Ph.D., CTRS, Jack Ciancio, M.A., RNC, and Tonia Russell for their constant support and encouragement throughout the development of this workbook.

A special thanks to the following Recreation Therapists: Peggy Cromer, Cecil Folk, Tim Clodfelter, and Ben Curti for their assistance in creating the case studies.

I'd like to thank Charlsena Stone, TRS/CTRS, and the University of North Carolina–Greensboro graduate and undergraduate students who took the time to pilot this material, and offered suggestions and encouragment.

And finally, to my parents, Joan and Mel, who have always encouraged me to set goals and achieve them.

Introduction to Writing Goals and Objectives

For several years now, I have worked with students and interns from around the country and witnessed firsthand their needs for further education on writing goals and objectives. It is evident that once taught basic techniques, students, interns, and entry-level professionals become more confident in developing goals and objectives for their clients and patients. Practice, practice, practice is what it takes to become equipped with the fundamentals of better documentation that will, in the long-run, serve the patient, recreation therapist, hospital, community setting, and outside reviewing organizations.

Many recreation therapists dread writing measurable goals and objectives for their patients or clients. In the beginning, writing goals and objectives can be frustrating, but with determination, instruction, and training, they will become easier to write.

The process of writing goals and objectives takes time, thought, consideration, and inclusion of the client or patient. This manual is designed to take recreation therapy students and entry-level professionals through a simple process of how to write measurable goals and objectives. The practice worksheets in this manual are designed to help build confidence.

Throughout this manual, patients and clients will be referred to only as patients.

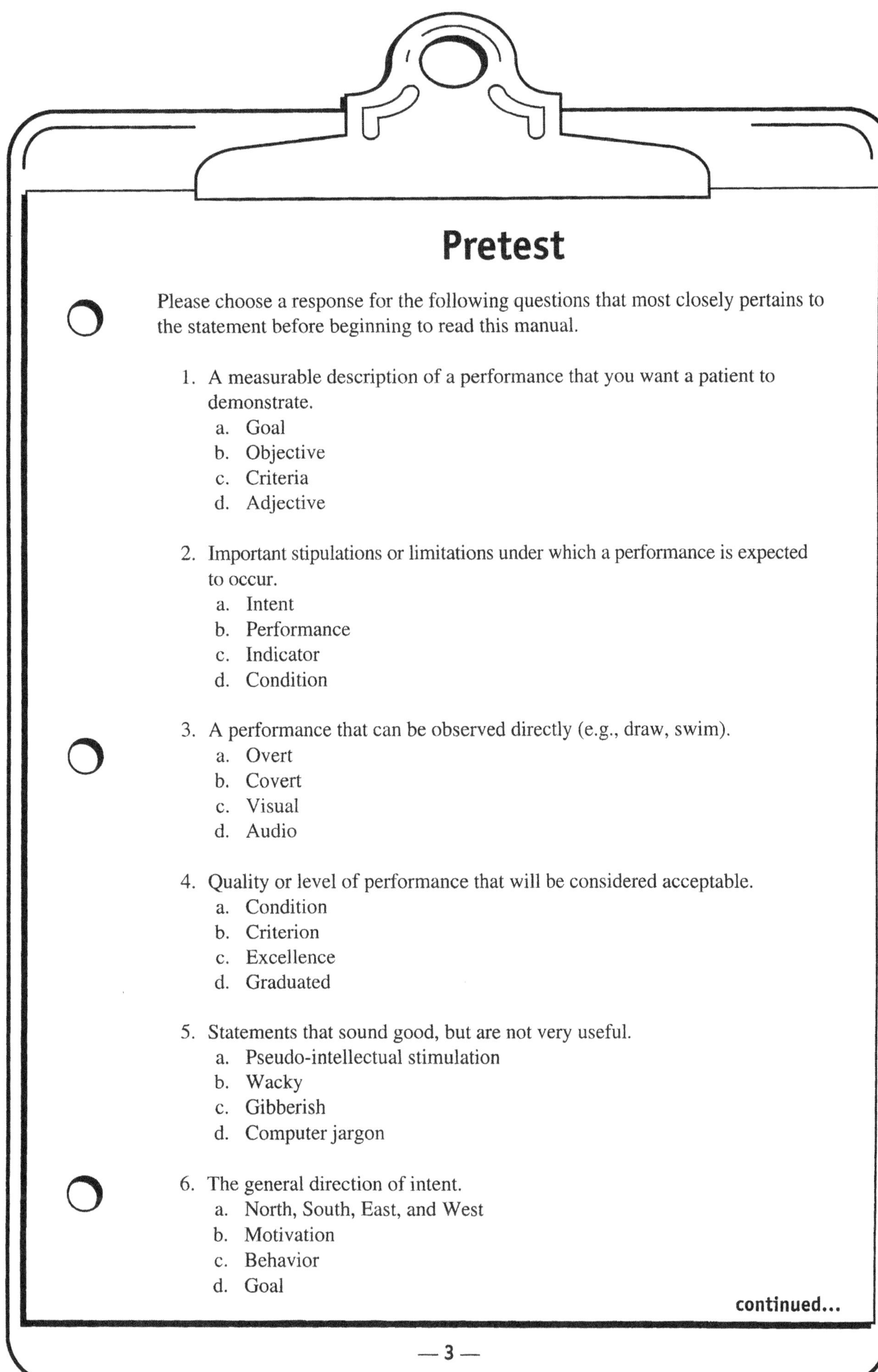

Pretest

Please choose a response for the following questions that most closely pertains to the statement before beginning to read this manual.

1. A measurable description of a performance that you want a patient to demonstrate.
   a. Goal
   b. Objective
   c. Criteria
   d. Adjective

2. Important stipulations or limitations under which a performance is expected to occur.
   a. Intent
   b. Performance
   c. Indicator
   d. Condition

3. A performance that can be observed directly (e.g., draw, swim).
   a. Overt
   b. Covert
   c. Visual
   d. Audio

4. Quality or level of performance that will be considered acceptable.
   a. Condition
   b. Criterion
   c. Excellence
   d. Graduated

5. Statements that sound good, but are not very useful.
   a. Pseudo-intellectual stimulation
   b. Wacky
   c. Gibberish
   d. Computer jargon

6. The general direction of intent.
   a. North, South, East, and West
   b. Motivation
   c. Behavior
   d. Goal

continued...

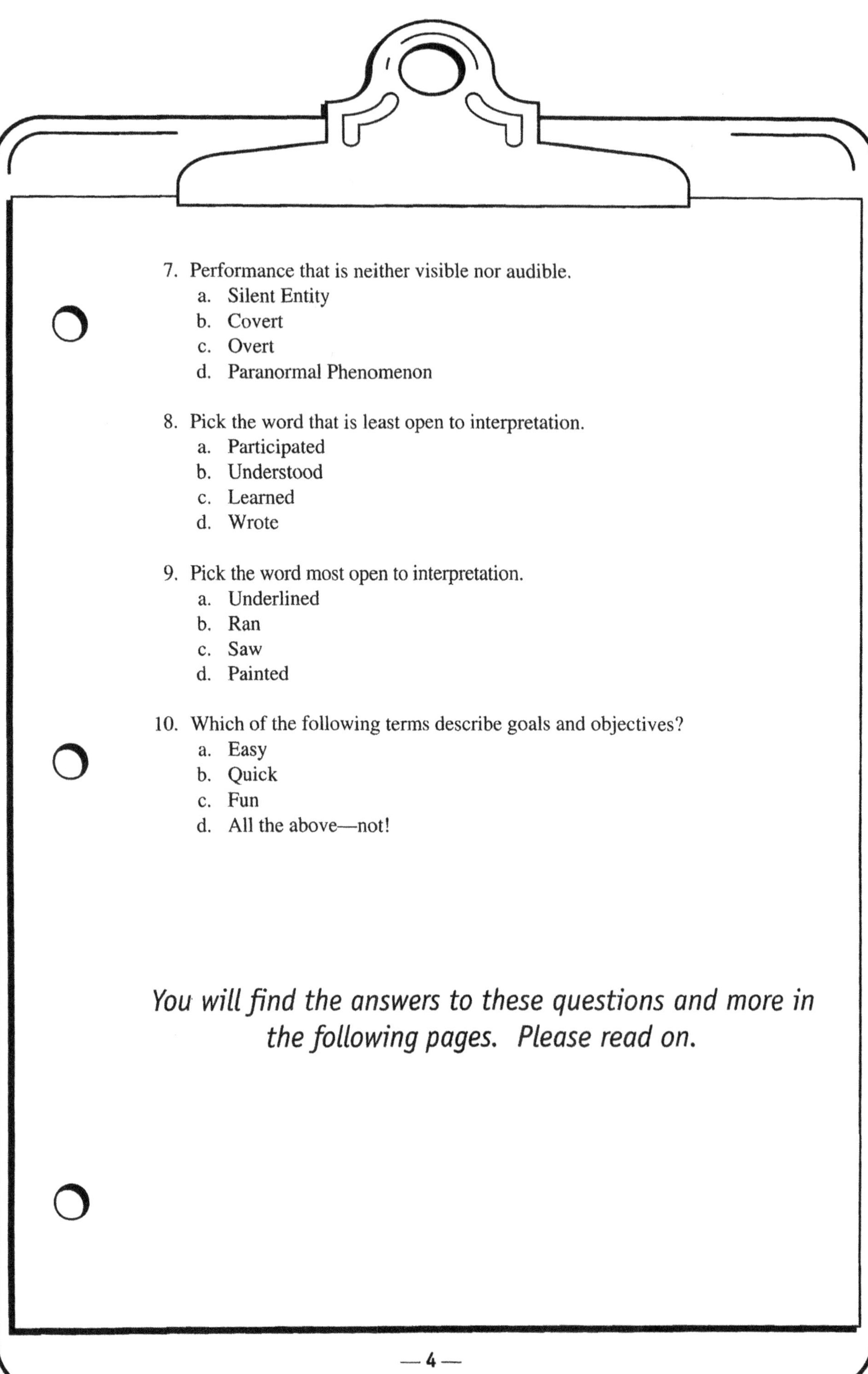

7. Performance that is neither visible nor audible.
    a. Silent Entity
    b. Covert
    c. Overt
    d. Paranormal Phenomenon

8. Pick the word that is least open to interpretation.
    a. Participated
    b. Understood
    c. Learned
    d. Wrote

9. Pick the word most open to interpretation.
    a. Underlined
    b. Ran
    c. Saw
    d. Painted

10. Which of the following terms describe goals and objectives?
    a. Easy
    b. Quick
    c. Fun
    d. All the above—not!

You will find the answers to these questions and more in the following pages. Please read on.

Why Is It Important to Write Goals and Objectives?

"Who says that it is important that recreation therapists write goals and objectives for their patients?" "Isn't it enough that I write out in protocols what my programs will do for patients?" "Who looks at the goals and objectives for each patient anyway?" These are all questions that recreation therapy students and professionals have asked at one time or another. Throughout this manual, answers to these questions, and more, will be provided.

Recreation therapy professionals agree that students and entry-level professionals need to practice documentation skills. Important steps in this process are making sure that the goals and objectives are "measurable, realistic, patient-orientated, and focused on outcomes." With the decrease in the length of stay at most hospitals, it is important to "coordinate goals with length of stay and to write goals that can be attained in this time frame." Acknowledging that length of stay is continuing to decrease, and insurance companies are focused on documentation for reimbursement, it is extremely important to recreation professionals to master the documentation issues, especially those of writing goals and objectives for their patients.

Many professionals believe that goals and objectives keep the treatment on target and measurable, and assist with justification of services. Without goals, recreation therapists would lack focus and would be unable to tell if treatment was effective. Practice, practice, and more practice makes the process of writing goals and objectives easier. Practice starts while still in school. During your practicum, observe the clinician's goals for patients. During internships, strive to write the best goals and objectives for your patients, and put these skills into practice as you move into the professional field.

Always attempt to include the patient in the development of his or her goals. Most insurance companies want to see that the patient is actively involved in his or her treatment process. Also, the patient will feel more control over his or her situation when included in goal development.

Assessments

Recreation therapists at all levels need an occasional reminder about the importance of conducting a thorough assessment. An assessment is the foundation from which the entire treatment plan is formulated, thus making the process of developing goals and objectives meaningful (see Figure 1).

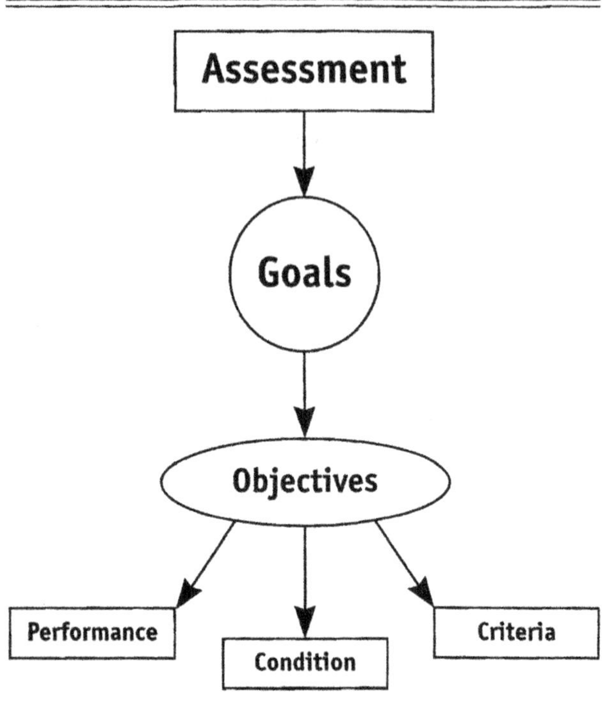

Figure 1 The assessment is the foundation of all patient goals and objectives.

The first step in developing goals and objectives is the assessment. Without a basic assessment, no legitimate goals or objectives can be written. This is evident in the fact that Peterson and Gunn dedicated an entire chapter to assessments in their book *Therapeutic Recreation Program Design* (1984, pp. 267–320). Recall that the therapeutic recreation process consists of four steps: assessment, planning, intervention, and evaluation [APIE] (Adams, 1995, p. 17; Austin and Crawford, 1991, p. 53).

The assessment provides a wealth of information that recreation therapists can utilize to understand the strengths and weaknesses of each patient and, in turn, develop appropriate goals and objectives that meet each patient's needs. Recreation therapists need to take time during the assessment phase to understand what the accurate needs of the patient are. The recreation therapist must communicate with the patient directly, or with family members if the patient is unable to answer for himself or herself. Next, the recreation therapist needs to use clinical skills to assist the patient in formulating realistic goals, to provide feedback during this process, and later to discuss achievement (Charboneau and Murphy, 1987; Grote et al., 1995; Peterson and Gunn, 1984; and Strecher et al., 1995). There are numerous assessment tools available to the recreation therapist (e.g., *Assessment Tools for Recreational Therapy: Red Book #1*, Idyll Arbor, Inc., 1997). Recreation therapists need to select the assessment tools that they are most confident in using, and that are the most reliable and valid. In this manual, the assumption will be that you are already aware of these tools and processes.

Meeting Patient Needs

The importance of quality goals and objectives documentation in the patients' charts has increased with the ever-changing reimbursement issues of insurance agencies. The length of stay for most patients has decreased, and organizations and agencies are looking to scale back services that do not assist the patients in meeting their [hospital] goal to get the patient out of the hospital sooner, while continuing to provide quality care. When you write goals and objectives

For Students...

Advice from a brief survey

A survey, given to recreation therapists about what advice they would give students concerning writing goals and objectives for patients, yielded no surprising results. Most recreation therapists encouraged students to "get ready to write, write, and write goals and objectives."

Recreation therapists also encouraged students to be attentive in class during the discussion of how to write goals and objectives; to remember that "goals and objectives keep the treatment on target, measurable and assist with justification of services;" and that "without goals you would not have a focus and would be unable to tell if treatment is effective."

with patients, their involvement helps them to focus their attention on their own most pressing needs. Along with that focus comes the hope that their own goals, upon achievement, will help get them out of the hospital sooner, and back to an optimum lifestyle.

Recreation therapy students and professionals must become comfortable, knowledgeable, and confident when writing goals and objectives. Writing effective goals and objectives also makes the process of documentation easier. The following pages and worksheets will help you develop the basic skills needed to write measurable goals and objectives.

An excellent resource to complement this manual is the book, *Preparing Instructional Objectives* by Robert Mager (1984). His text is based on instructional objectives. Mager's process involves stating a goal in broad terms (i.e., "increase assertiveness" or "improve physical functioning"). The objectives are then developed, and are more specific and directed toward achieving the goal (see Figure 2).

> **Goal:** General direction of intent; aim.
> **Objective:**
> Measurable description of a performance you want the patient to demonstrate; how to reach the goal.
>
> **Goal:** To reach the top of Hiker's Mountain.
> **Objective:**
> Patient will walk up Hiker's Mountain trail unassisted, from the starting marker to the marker at the top of the mountain. Patient will complete task in 1 hour or less.

The climber has a goal of making it to the top of Hiker's Mountain. There are a variety of ways this goal can be achieved, such as biking, walking, or flying. You, the practitioner, need to have a clear idea in your own mind of exactly what it is you want your patient to do and how you want it done. If you do not understand the goals and objectives, assume that your patient will not either. Also, goals and objectives must be developed with the patient, or else the goal will never be attained. If a goal is set by someone else and the patient has not accepted that goal as his or her own, or if the patient has not assisted in the development of a goal, then it is more than likely that the patient will not attain that goal.

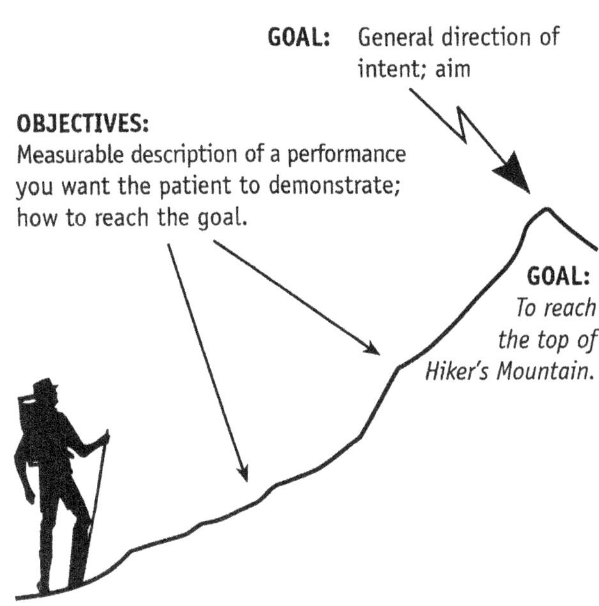

OBJECTIVE:
Patient will walk up Hiker's Mountain trail unassisted, from the starting marker to the marker at the top of the mountain. Patient will complete task in 1 hour or less.

Figure 2 **Hiker's Mountain:** A visual example of goal and objectives (Contributed by Tonia Russell)

Goals and Objectives

Writing goals and objectives so that they are concise and easy to understand requires parameters. Lee, Locke, and Latham define a goal as "that which one wants to accomplish; it concerns a valued, future end state" (Strecher et al., 1995, p. 191). An easy formula to remember is:

Goal = *Broad Statement + Intent*

Recreation therapists utilize an assessment in the process of developing individualized goals for their patients. Developing the goal is accomplished with the patient's agreement or input. If the patient is unable to state his or her goal then the family members are consulted. The formation of a goal gives a clear end point to what needs to be accomplished.

An example of a goal is: Patient will increase stress management skills within two weeks. This example gives both the patient and the therapist a clear outcome for the patient to accomplish. The direction is broad in the above example, therefore, the next step is to develop stepping stones so the patient can reach the goal. These stepping stones are known as objectives.

Objectives are more specific than goals. An objective is a measurable description of a performance you want a patient to be able to demonstrate. Goals are stated broadly and the objective is specific—and several objectives may be required to reach one goal. Some recreation therapists select one objective to begin the steps toward the goal. Upon completion of one objective they then develop another objective. Mager (1984) utilized this method of writing quality objectives: the objective must contain the performance, condition, and criteria. The *performance* is what the patient is expected to do. The *condition* is under what limitation or circumstances the performance is to occur. The *criteria* states qualities that determine if the performance was achieved, and how you will know the performance was accomplished. Remember this easy formula:

Objective = ***Performance* + *Condition* + *Criteria***

If one of these components is lacking, then the objective is incomplete. These three components are the tributaries of every major objective.

In looking at the performance aspect, you can assume you will need a verb, either a doing verb (overt) or a being verb (covert). It is important to select verbs carefully and specifically to meet what it is you are expecting in the performance. The verbs that you decide to use in your objective must be specific and open to little or no misinterpretation. Further discussion of each of these terms will be discussed later (see Analysis of Verb Usage, p. 9).

There are no absolutes in dealing with writing goals and objectives; however, the worksheets that follow will offer a foundation for writing technically correct goals and objectives. It is important for you to proofread your work. It can be helpful to let others proofread as well. Better yet, you or another person should read them aloud. They not only can spot spelling and grammatical errors, but also can offer you their interpretation of the objective. If their understanding of what you meant is totally different from yours, rewrite it. If the goals and objectives are not clear, this could lead to them being misunderstood by other professionals who read them, including insurance companies. The insurance companies may choose not to reimburse you for your services if the patient's goals and objectives are unclear. You also want to write an objective that any therapist could accurately implement in your absence.

In the beginning, writing goals and objectives can be frustrating, but with practice, objectives will become clearer and easier to write. The worksheets in this manual will help you begin this process.

As the recreation therapy field continues to grow, so does the prospect that additional goal-writing techniques will be developed. Today's practitioners are increasingly challenged to meet the needs of not only the patient, but also that of accrediting bodies and third-party reimbursing agencies. It will be your choice when selecting the guidelines most appropriate for developing your patient's goals and objectives. This manual offers a step-by-step approach to writing measurable goals and objectives. The worksheets address the most common areas of identification of content for acceptable goals and objectives. They allow you to practice writing goals and objectives from case studies that have suggested goals and objectives as examples. You will also find abbreviations, recommended resources, and references at the end of the manual.

Terminology

The following terms are specific to the process of writing goals and objectives. You will see these terms throughout this manual and hopefully will incorporate these into your clinical vocabulary.

Goal: The result or achievement toward which the effort is directed; aim; end (*Webster's Dictionary, 9th edition,* 1984); the broad statement of intent.

Objective: A measurable description of a performance you want the patient to demonstrate; the outcome. Objectives are specific and contain the performance, condition, and criterion/criteria needed to transform the goal into a measurable end.

Performance: What the patient is expected to be able to do in very specific terms.

Condition: Important circumstances or limitations under which the performance is expected to occur.

Criterion/criteria: States qualities that determine if the performance was achieved, or how you will know if the performance was accomplished.

Overt: Performance that can be observed directly, whether that performance is visible or audible (Mager, 1984, p. 43).

Covert: Performance that cannot be observed directly; performance that is mental, invisible, cognitive, or internal...it can only be detected by asking someone to say something, or to do something visible (Mager, 1984, p. 43).

Indicator Behavior: Used in conjunction with a covert performance statement, it is a visible performance that will allow you to determine whether the covert performance has been accomplished.

Intent: Your purpose or your goal.

Gibberish: Statements that are too wordy. They may sound good, but they are not very useful.

Analysis of Verb Usage

Like Mager, Beitz (1996) reminds individuals to be careful of their verb usage. There are some verbs that are easy to evaluate objectively, such as run, walk, hike, draw, write, speak, and blink. Some verbs are open to interpretation, and their specific meaning is misunderstood, such as "comprehend." *Comprehend* can mean anything from listening to the rules of a checker game to being able to play a game of checkers without prompting. "We do not see a person analyze a poem; we see or hear a report of his or her analysis." This is another example of the importance of selecting verbs to eliminate confusion (Kibler, Barker, and Miles, 1970, p. 20).

Verbs are important when writing the performance you want the patient to demonstrate. Reminiscent of grammar school, some verbs need helpers or indicator behaviors. Being verbs, or passive verbs, such as *appreciate, learn, feel* or *state,* are open to many interpretations. It is permissible to use them in an objective, but often your intent may be unclear. If you choose to use a "being verb," adding an indicator relieves that confusion.

Overt or Doing Words: Used in an objective. The patient is either performing the task or not performing the task. Terms are concise and specific.

Writing
Running
Drawing
Eating
Sewing
Underlining

Covert or Being Words: Not to be used alone in an objective. These words are open to interpretation.

Appreciating
Understanding
Knowing
Feeling
Enthusiastic
Being
Enjoy

Practice #1: Identifying Overt and Covert Words

Below are a few examples of overt and covert performances. Place a check mark beside the overt performance that can stand alone. If the performance is covert (a performance that cannot be observed directly), write the simplest indicator that you can think of to make it measurable and open to the least amount of interpretation.

1. Identify leisure preference. ____________________

   ____

2. Play the piano. ____________________

   ____

3. Demonstrate appropriate social skills. ____________________

   ____

4. Distinguish assertive behavior from passive and aggressive behaviors. __

   ____

5. Recall daily schedule. ____________________

   ____

6. Walk one mile. ____________________

   ____

7. Express feelings. ____________________

   ____

8. Establish goals. ____________________

   ____

continued...

9. State leisure interest. ____

____

10. Understand the rules of volleyball. ________________________________

____

Answers to Practice #1: Identifying Overt and Covert Words

The following are possible responses to the question of whether the performance is covert or overt. Remember that overt terms are observed directly, whether that performance is audible or visible (detected by the ear or the eye). Covert terms cannot be observed directly, and are performances that are mental, invisible, cognitive, or internal. The covert performances can only be determined by the therapist asking the patient to do something visible or to say something. The covert terms have been corrected by adding an indicator behavior. Remember that indicator behavior should be a term that is visible or audible, and allows you to determine whether the covert performance has been accomplished.

1. *Identify leisure preference*: Covert.
   The term identify is open to interpretation. You can alter the wording to "The patient will verbally identify leisure preference" or change the covert term to simply "Patient will verbalize leisure preference."
2. *Play the piano*: Overt.
   You can easily determine if the patient plays the piano in any way, shape, or form, he or she has meet this performance objective. You can both see and hear this performance.
3. *Demonstrate appropriate social skills*: Covert.
   What one therapist may feel is appropriate, another therapist may not. It is important to state specifically what it is you want to see happen. For example, "Patient will not yell during group participation;" "Patient will speak calmly;" "Patient will not threaten others."
4. *Distinguish assertive behavior from passive and aggressive behaviors*: Covert.
   This performance is close, but you don't know how the therapist wants this task to be done, verbally, in writing, or during a role-play. "Patient will verbalize the difference between assertive, aggressive, and passive behaviors."
5. *Recall daily schedule*: Covert.
   I could recall the schedule in my mind, but you would not be able to measure this. "Patient will state when asked by therapist what his or her schedule is for the day."

6. *Walk one mile*: Overt.
   This performance is easily measured. Walking is a visible action that can be measured. It is either done or not done.
7. *Express feelings*: Covert.
   How do you want them to do this? "Patient will write in his or her journal daily feelings." "Patient, when asked, will state his or her feelings at that time."
8. *Establish goals*: Covert.
   How do you want the patient to establish them: in writing, on a tape recorder, verbally to you, in the form of a drawing?
9. *State leisure interest*: Covert.
   This sounds good, but it is not clear what *state* means. "Patient will verbally state" or "Patient will state in writing what his or her leisure interests are."
10. *Understand the rules of volleyball*: Covert.
    Remember you cannot read the patient's mind to ascertain if he or she can "understand" or not. You can, however see their participation in a game and determine if they are following the rules. Here again, you are having to ask the patient to do something else, so therefore the performance is covert. "Patient will play one game of volleyball following the rules as previously discussed by therapist." "Patient will verbalize three rules in the game of volleyball."

What Is a Goal?

Goals are broad statements of intent; the overall direction that you desire your patient to work toward. The goal is discussed and developed with the patient. Possible goals are:

- To increase functional leisure skills
- To increase leisure awareness
- To increase social interaction
- To complete community reintegration program
- To increase awareness of stress management techniques
- To increase awareness of relaxation methods
- To increase assertiveness
- To increase anger management skills
- To decrease physical aggression
- To decrease verbal outbursts
- To improve time management skills
- To maintain cognitive level
- To develop discharge plan

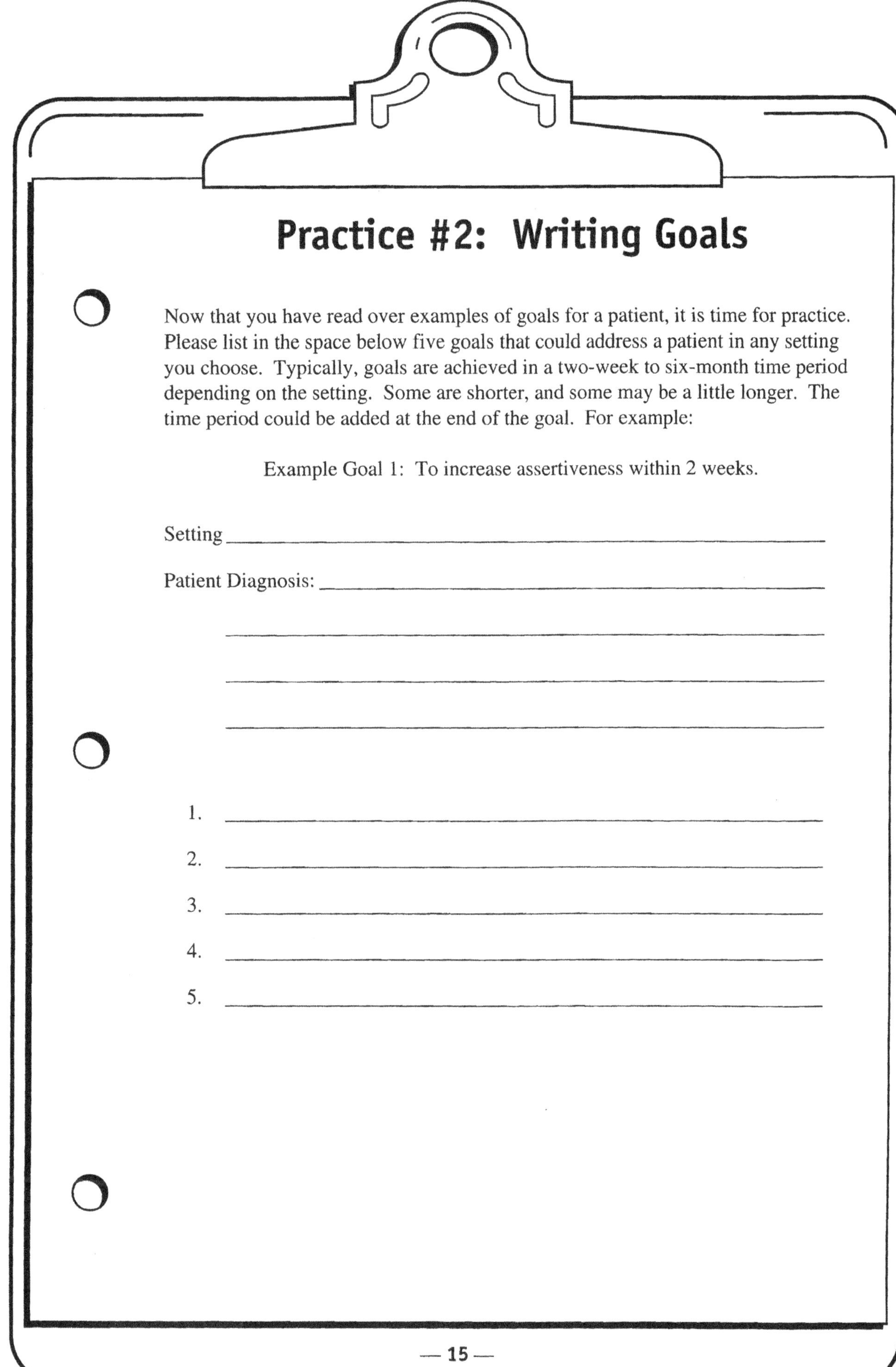

Practice #2: Writing Goals

Now that you have read over examples of goals for a patient, it is time for practice. Please list in the space below five goals that could address a patient in any setting you choose. Typically, goals are achieved in a two-week to six-month time period depending on the setting. Some are shorter, and some may be a little longer. The time period could be added at the end of the goal. For example:

Example Goal 1: To increase assertiveness within 2 weeks.

Setting ____

Patient Diagnosis: __________________________________

1. ____
2. ____
3. ____
4. ____
5. ____

Questions to Ponder about Objectives

As you prepare to write goals and objectives there are a few things that you will want to remember. Goals are stated in broad terms. Objectives are the steps necessary to achieve the goal. An objective must include a performance, condition, and a list of criteria. To make sure these exist you can ask the following questions to test your objective:

1. "What is the main intent of the objective?"
2. "What does the learner have to do to demonstrate achievement of the objective?"
3. "What will the learner have to do it with, or to it? And what, if anything, will the learner have to do without?"
4. "How will we know when the performance is good enough to be considered acceptable?" (Mager, 1984, p. 86)

Asking questions of your objective will help to work out any problems and make it easy for anyone reading your objective to understand what is expected.

What Is an Objective?

The objective is a measurable description of a performance you want a patient to demonstrate. The objective is the stepping stone toward reaching the goal. The objective requires three specific parts to make it functional—the performance, condition, and criteria. As with the goal, the objective(s) must be discussed with the patient. An example of a goal and objective with its necessary components is offered below:

Goal 1.0: To increase assertiveness by 2 weeks.
Objective 1.1:
Patient will attend three classes on assertiveness within one week.

So, what are the components of this objective?

Performance: "Patient will attend..."

- The 'patient will attend' is what he or she is expected to demonstrate.

Condition: "...three classes on assertiveness..."

- Circumstances under which the patient must perform

Criteria: "...within one week."

- The quality of the performance that must be demonstrated in order for the objective to be achieved.

Asking questions of your objective will help to work out any problems and make it easy for anyone to understand what is expected.

Practice #3: Identifying the Performance

Your task is to review each of the following statements and determine if they include a performance. Circle "Yes" if the statement includes a performance. Circle "No" if the statement is without a performance. Remember to ask questions—Does each at least tell what the patient will be doing when demonstrating achievement of the objective? Are you clear on what is being asked by each statement?

1. Understand the principles of sportsmanship. Yes No
2. Patient will name the bones of the body. Yes No
3. Know the needs for nursing care associated with the stressors of life situations and with common aspects of illness. Yes No
4. Patient will identify (circle) objectives that include a statement of desired performance. Yes No
5. Appreciate the ability of others, and perform as an intelligent spectator. Yes No

Answers to Practice #3: Identifying the Performance

There are several statements below that are unclear and, therefore, open to misinterpretation of their meaning of the desired performance.

1. Understand the principles of sportsmanship.
   Yes **NO**

Comment: What is meant by "understand?" It would be better for the patient to state (verbally) three qualities needed that demonstrate good sportsmanship.

2. Patient will name the bones of the body.
   YES No

Comment: How is the patient expected to "name" the bones of the body? Does he or she need to verbalize or write them?

3. Know the needs for nursing care associated with the stressors of life situations and with common aspects of illness.
   Yes **NO**

Comment: This statement sounds good, but says nothing. It is gibberish.

4. Patient will identify (circle) objectives that include a statement of desired performance.
   YES No

Comment: The patient is expected to circle. This is visible.

5. Appreciate the ability of others, and perform as an intelligent spectator.
   Yes **NO**

Comment: How can you tell if someone is appreciating? How can you measure appreciation? What would your suggestion be for rewriting this performance?

Practice #4: Is It a Useful Objective?

Read the objectives below. Place a check mark in the appropriate column to indicate any components that are useful in the objective. If the component is unclear, leave the column blank.

Performance | Condition | Criteria

1. Demonstrate a knowledge of the principles of tennis.

2. Patient will write an essay on their feelings.

3. On the 25-yard range, draw your service revolver and fire five rounds from the hip within 3 seconds. At 25 yards all rounds must hit the standard silhouette target.

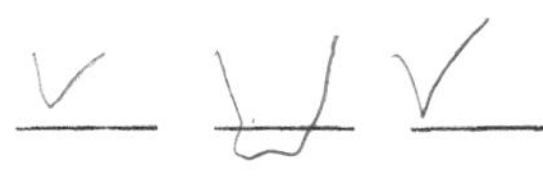

4. Patient will know the rules of wheelchair basketball well.

5. Given verbal instruction of the steps to deep breathing, patient will demonstrate three deep breaths by the end of one relaxation class.

Answers to Practice #4: Is It a Useful Objective?

Remember, areas that are left blank are missing components to your objective. What would make it acceptable? Below you will find possible suggestions:

	Perf	*Cond*	*Crit*
1. Demonstrate a knowledge of the principles of tennis.	__	__	__

All components are missing. This is too vague. What one therapist might accept as knowledge of the principles of tennis may not be the same as another therapist. Example, one therapist may interpret this as the patient verbally stating the principles (some or all), and another might need to see the patient demonstrate the principles (some or all). What is the time frame and under what condition?

2. Patient will write an essay on their feelings.	X	__	__

The performance is stated, the patient must "write." The other components are lacking.

3. On the 25-yard range, draw your service revolver and fire five rounds from the hip within 3 seconds. At 25 yards all rounds must hit the standard silhouette target.	X	X	X

All components are present and it is clear what has to be demonstrated.

4. Patient will know the rules of wheelchair basketball well.	__	__	__

This is gibberish. It sounds pretty good but says nothing of value. How could you write it to be more complete? Try it now:

____

____

5. Given verbal instruction of the steps to deep breathing, patient will demonstrate three deep breaths by the end of one relaxation class.	X	X	X

It is easy to account for this objective being attained; it is clear and concise.

Practice #5: Goals and Objectives

In the following examples, you are to write in the space provided whether or not these goals and objectives are measurable. Do they include performance, condition, and criteria? If they have all the components of a functional objective, then place a check mark by the component. If one of the components is missing, then write in the space provided what would make it functional. Take your time. You can look back at the terminology section to recall definitions of terms.

Goal: Foster awareness of personal value system.
Objective:
Given a list of 20 values, patient will rank (write) values in order of importance, with one indicating most important and 20 indicating least important. Patient will complete task during one-hour session.

Performance ____

Condition ____

Criteria ____

____

Goal: Develop assertion skills.
Objective:
During a role-playing situation, patient will demonstrate appropriate assertiveness skills.

Performance ____

Condition ____

Criteria ____

____

continued...

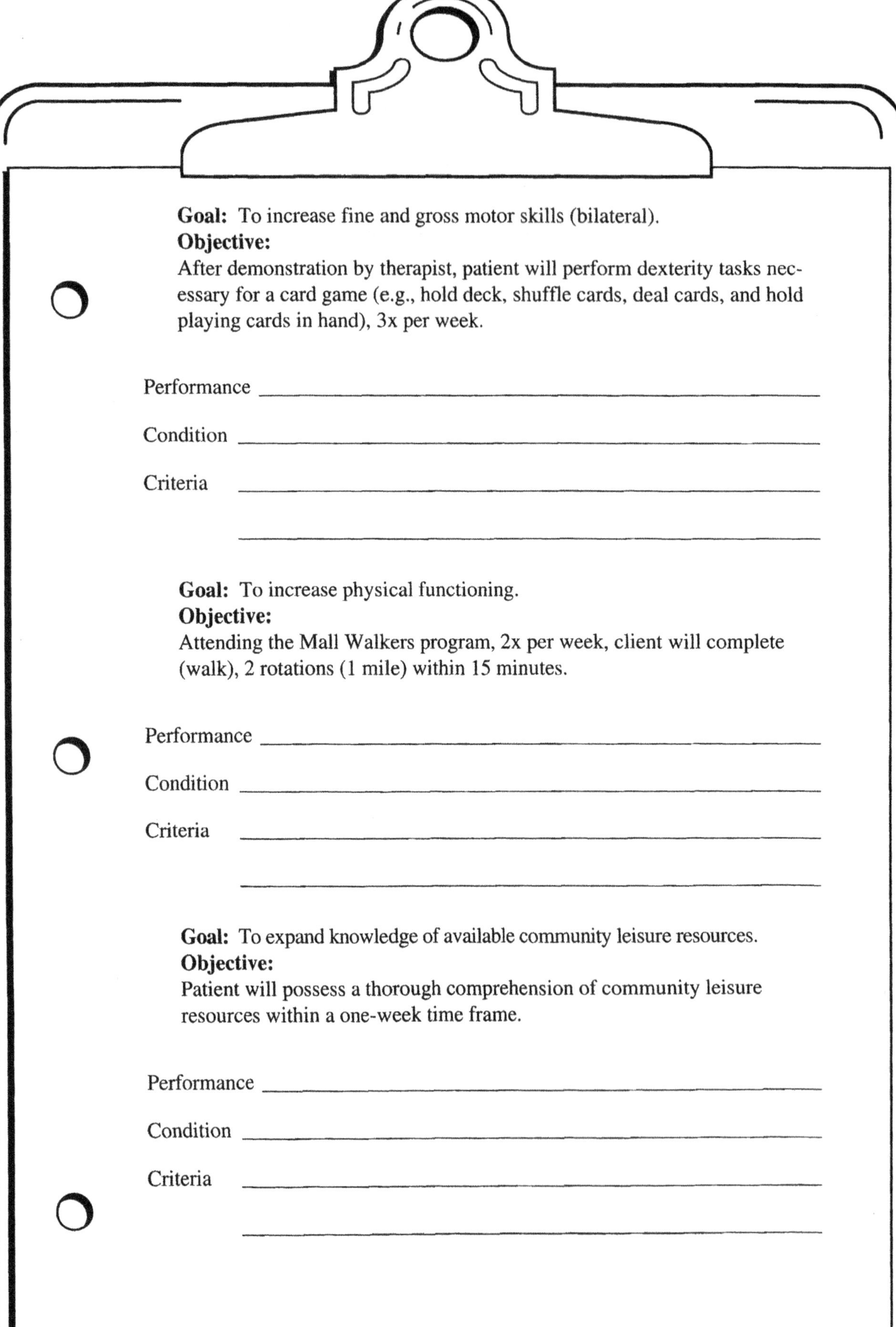

Goal: To increase fine and gross motor skills (bilateral).
Objective:
After demonstration by therapist, patient will perform dexterity tasks necessary for a card game (e.g., hold deck, shuffle cards, deal cards, and hold playing cards in hand), 3x per week.

Performance ______________________________

Condition ______________________________

Criteria ______________________________

____

Goal: To increase physical functioning.
Objective:
Attending the Mall Walkers program, 2x per week, client will complete (walk), 2 rotations (1 mile) within 15 minutes.

Performance ______________________________

Condition ______________________________

Criteria ______________________________

____

Goal: To expand knowledge of available community leisure resources.
Objective:
Patient will possess a thorough comprehension of community leisure resources within a one-week time frame.

Performance ______________________________

Condition ______________________________

Criteria ______________________________

____

Answers to Practice #5: Goals and Objectives

Please notice that some of the language has changed in order to make the objectives measurable.

Goal: Foster awareness of personal value system.
Objective:
Given a list of 20 values [*condition*], patient will rank (write) [*performance*] values in order of importance, with 1 indicating most important and 20 indicating least important. Patient will complete task during one-hour session [*criterion*].

Goal: Develop assertion skills.
Objective:
During a role-playing situation [*condition*], patient will deny [*performance*] a request from a peer in three tries [*criterion*].

Goal: To increase fine and gross motor skills (bilateral).
Objective:
After demonstration by therapist [*condition*], patient will perform [*performance*] dexterity tasks necessary for a card game (e.g., hold deck, shuffle cards, deal cards, and hold playing cards in hand) 3x per week [*criterion*].

Goal: To improve cardiovascular status.
Objective:
Attending the Mall Walkers program 2x per week [*condition*], patient will complete (walk) [*performance*] 2 rotations (1 mile) within 15 minutes [*criterion*].

Goal: To expand knowledge of available community leisure resources.
Objective:
Given a local telephone book [*condition*], patient will be able to list [*performance*] a minimum of five community leisure resources within a one-week time frame [*criterion*].

Case Examples

The following pages will provide you with the opportunity to practice identifying the patient's needs from assessments. You need to write at least two goals and objectives for each case. Abbreviations of terms follow.

Remember to include the performance, condition, and criteria in each of your objectives. You are practicing under the premise of not actually speaking to the patient—remember, in real life situations you should involve the patient in this process. All cases involve fictitious information—any similarities with real patients are strictly coincidental.

Selected Abbreviations

AA	Alcoholics Anonymous
ABI	Acute brain injury
ADLs	Activities of daily living
Adm.	Admission
BSA	Body surface area
c/o	Complained of
Dx	Diagnosis
ETOH	Ethyl alcohol
Hx	History
Liabilities	Weakness
L5	Lumbar fifth region
LE	Lower extremity
lt.	Left
Memory book	Memory book (provides information for patient)
mo	Month
MVA	Motor vehicle accident
Pt.	Patient
PMHx	Past medical history
rt.	Right
TBSA	Total body surface area
UE	Upper extremity
wk	Week
x	Times; approximately; about
yo	Years old

Demographic Abbreviations

A	Asian	H	Hispanic
B	Black	W	White
M	Male	F	Female
S	Single	D	Divorced

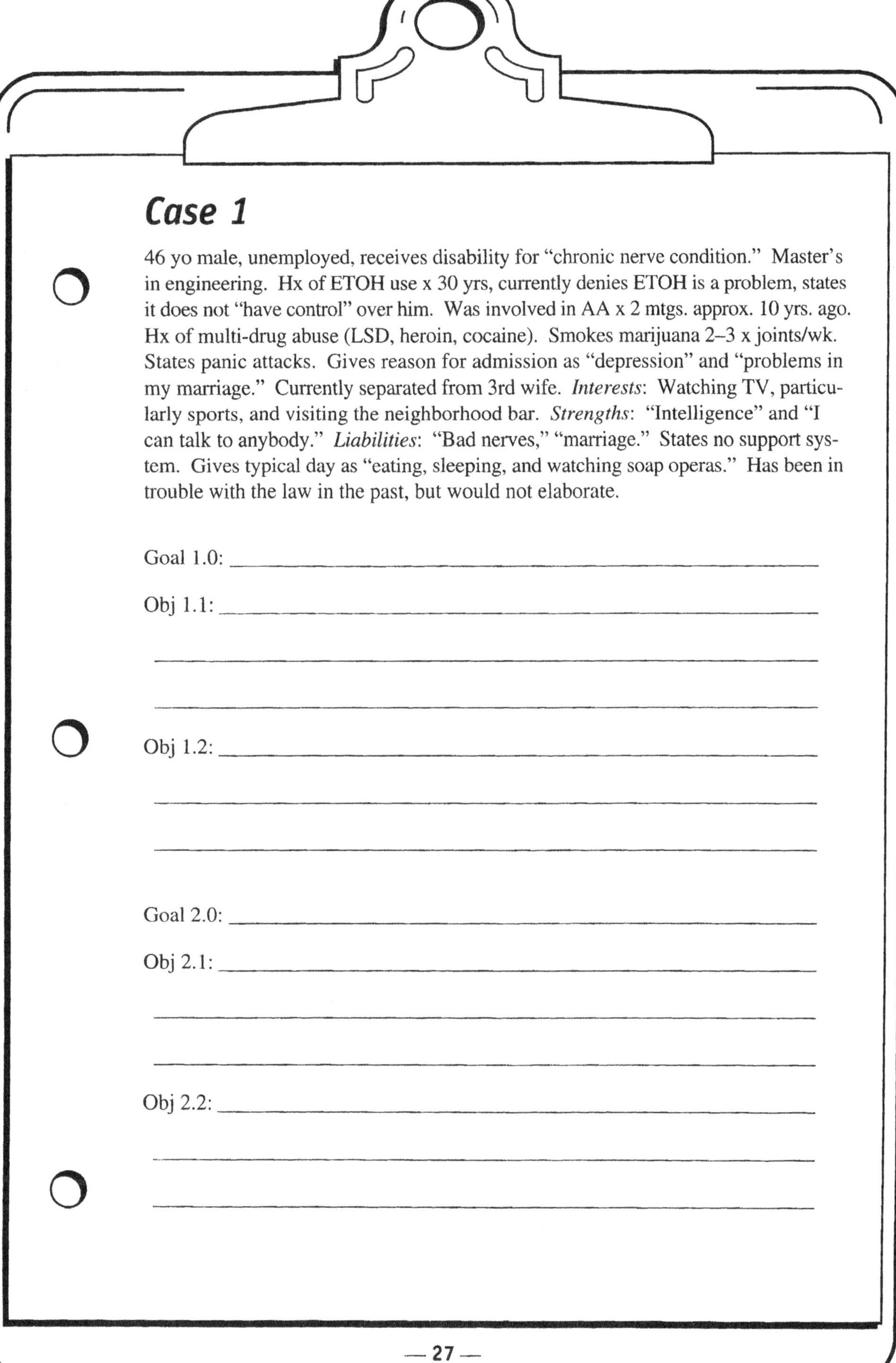

Case 1

46 yo male, unemployed, receives disability for "chronic nerve condition." Master's in engineering. Hx of ETOH use x 30 yrs, currently denies ETOH is a problem, states it does not "have control" over him. Was involved in AA x 2 mtgs. approx. 10 yrs. ago. Hx of multi-drug abuse (LSD, heroin, cocaine). Smokes marijuana 2–3 x joints/wk. States panic attacks. Gives reason for admission as "depression" and "problems in my marriage." Currently separated from 3rd wife. *Interests*: Watching TV, particularly sports, and visiting the neighborhood bar. *Strengths*: "Intelligence" and "I can talk to anybody." *Liabilities*: "Bad nerves," "marriage." States no support system. Gives typical day as "eating, sleeping, and watching soap operas." Has been in trouble with the law in the past, but would not elaborate.

Goal 1.0: ______________________________

Obj 1.1: ______________________________

____

____

Obj 1.2: ______________________________

____

____

Goal 2.0: ______________________________

Obj 2.1: ______________________________

____

____

Obj 2.2: ______________________________

____

____

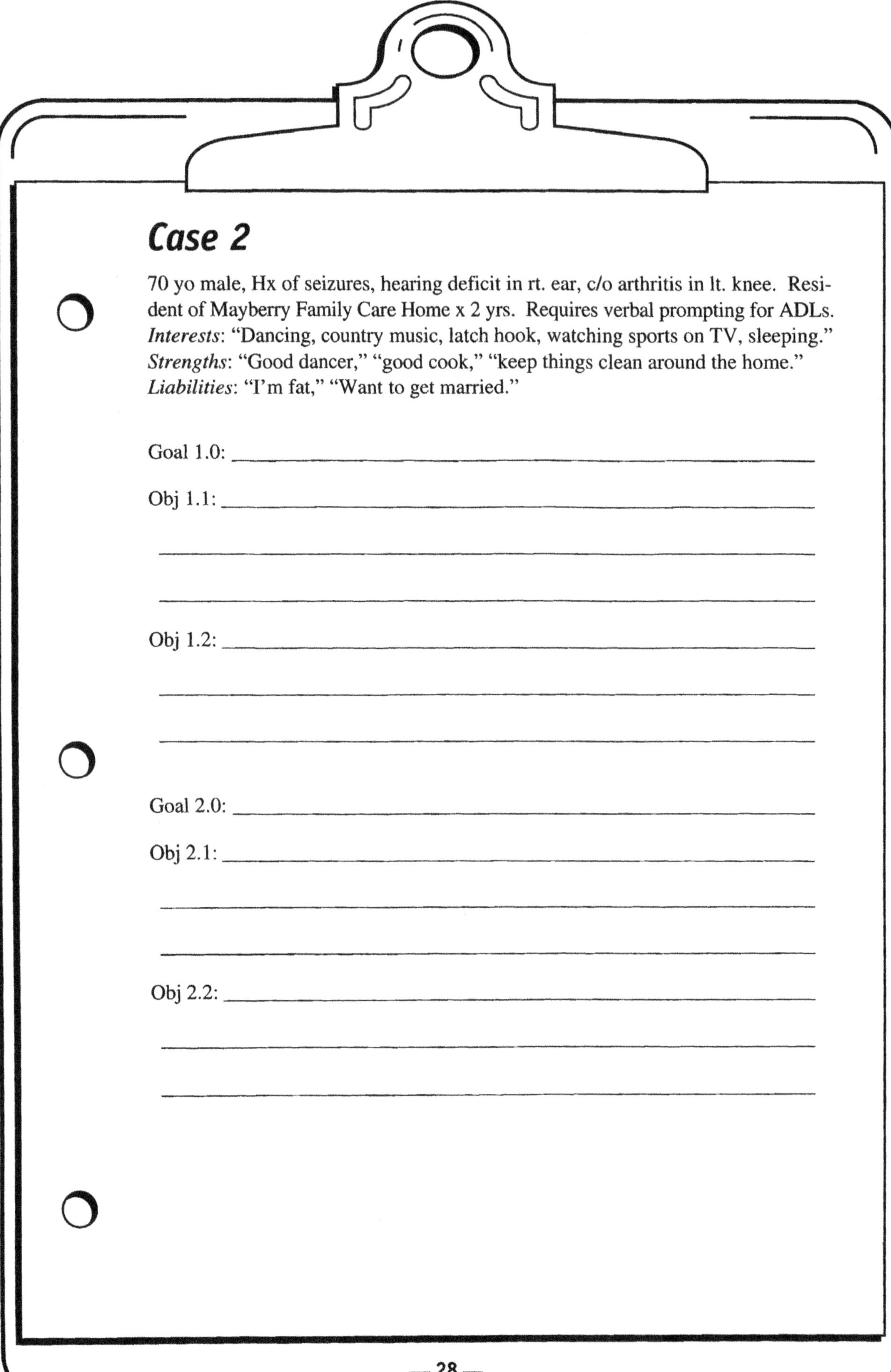

Case 2

70 yo male, Hx of seizures, hearing deficit in rt. ear, c/o arthritis in lt. knee. Resident of Mayberry Family Care Home x 2 yrs. Requires verbal prompting for ADLs.
Interests: "Dancing, country music, latch hook, watching sports on TV, sleeping."
Strengths: "Good dancer," "good cook," "keep things clean around the home."
Liabilities: "I'm fat," "Want to get married."

Goal 1.0: ______________________________

Obj 1.1: ______________________________

____

____

Obj 1.2: ______________________________

____

____

Goal 2.0: ______________________________

Obj 2.1: ______________________________

____

____

Obj 2.2: ______________________________

____

____

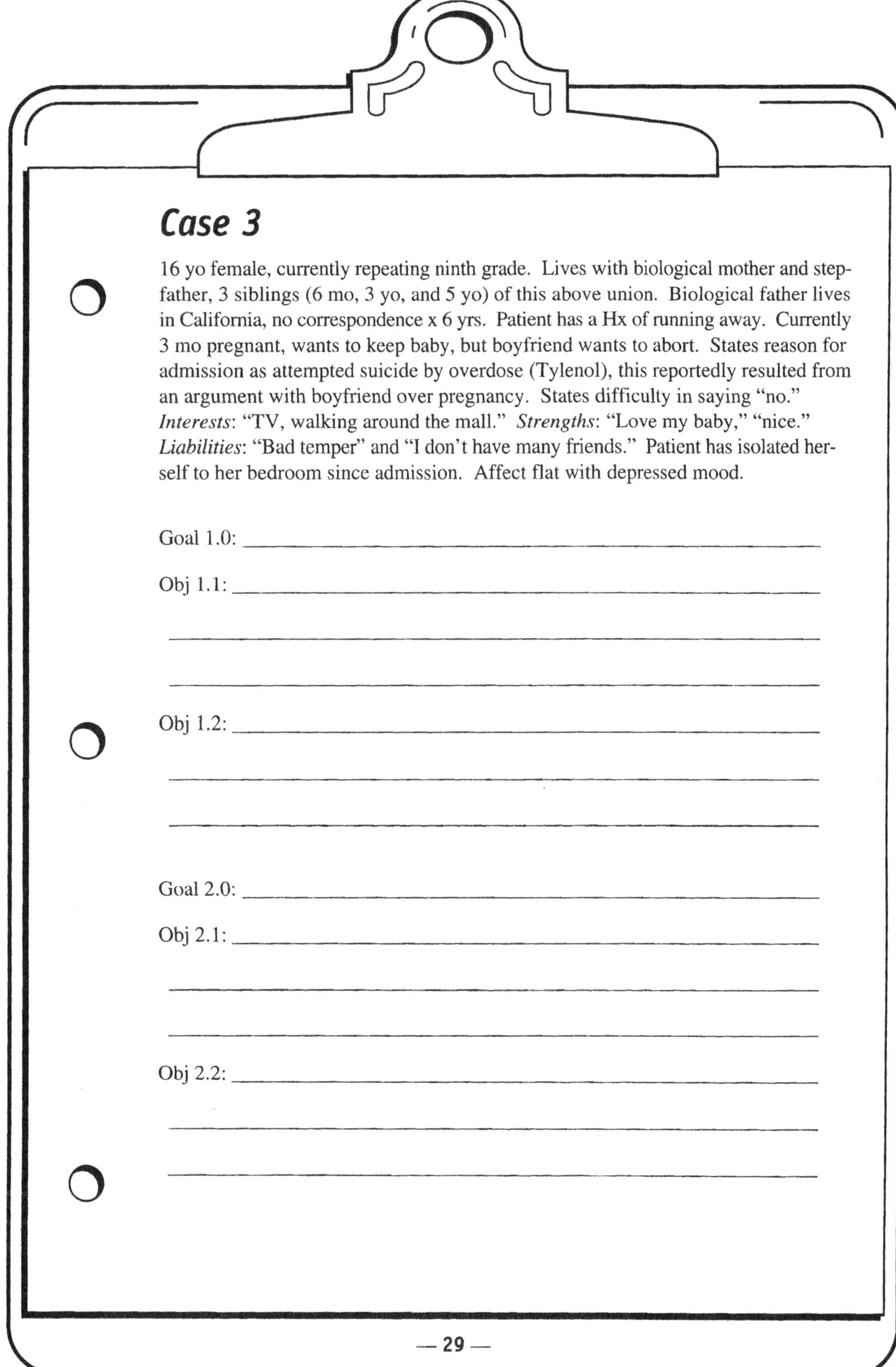

Case 3

16 yo female, currently repeating ninth grade. Lives with biological mother and stepfather, 3 siblings (6 mo, 3 yo, and 5 yo) of this above union. Biological father lives in California, no correspondence x 6 yrs. Patient has a Hx of running away. Currently 3 mo pregnant, wants to keep baby, but boyfriend wants to abort. States reason for admission as attempted suicide by overdose (Tylenol), this reportedly resulted from an argument with boyfriend over pregnancy. States difficulty in saying "no." *Interests*: "TV, walking around the mall." *Strengths*: "Love my baby," "nice." *Liabilities*: "Bad temper" and "I don't have many friends." Patient has isolated herself to her bedroom since admission. Affect flat with depressed mood.

Goal 1.0: ____________________

Obj 1.1: ____________________

____

____

Obj 1.2: ____________________

____

____

Goal 2.0: ____________________

Obj 2.1: ____________________

____

____

Obj 2.2: ____________________

____

____

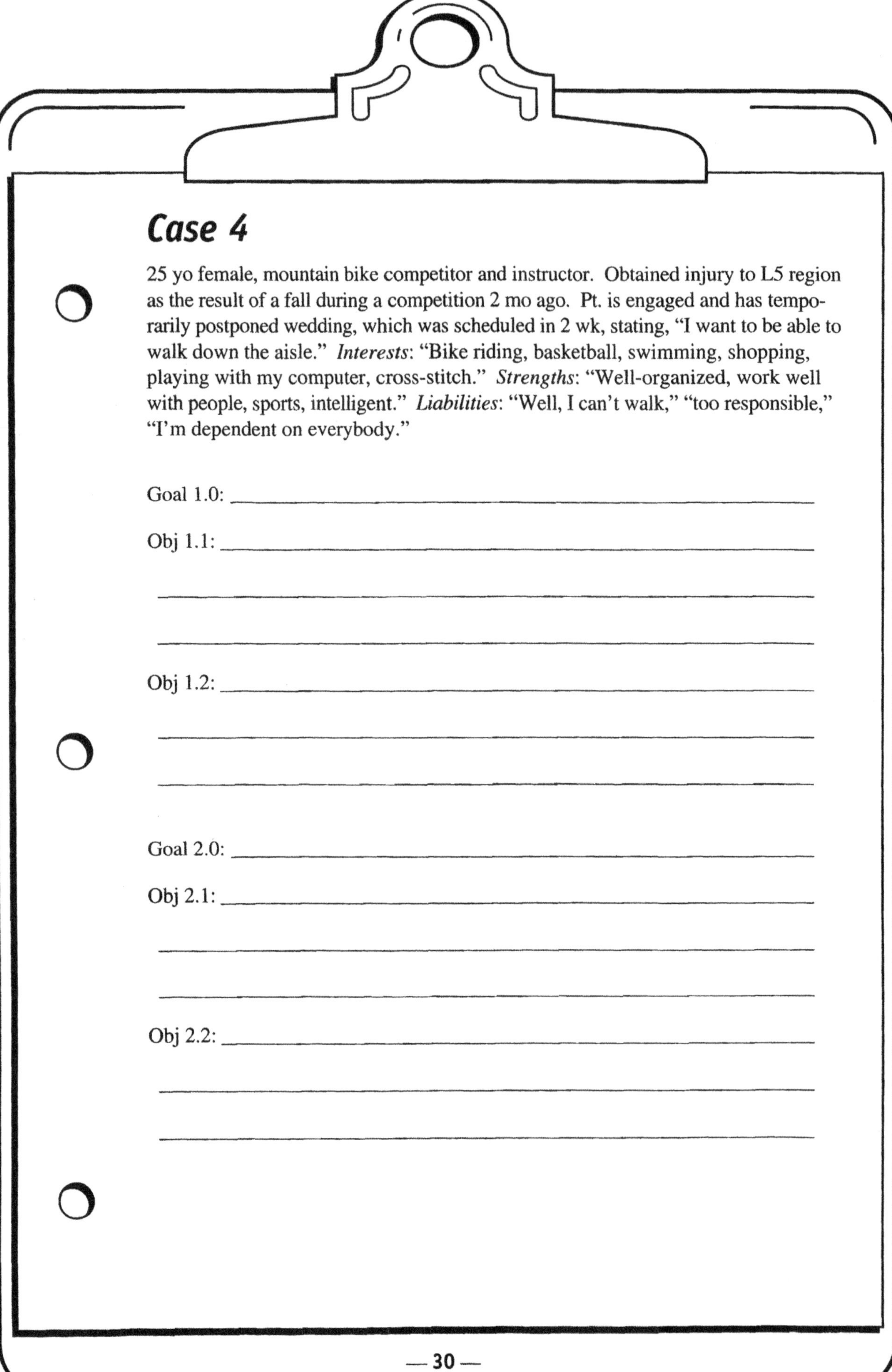

Case 4

25 yo female, mountain bike competitor and instructor. Obtained injury to L5 region as the result of a fall during a competition 2 mo ago. Pt. is engaged and has temporarily postponed wedding, which was scheduled in 2 wk, stating, "I want to be able to walk down the aisle." *Interests*: "Bike riding, basketball, swimming, shopping, playing with my computer, cross-stitch." *Strengths*: "Well-organized, work well with people, sports, intelligent." *Liabilities*: "Well, I can't walk," "too responsible," "I'm dependent on everybody."

Goal 1.0: ____________________

Obj 1.1: ____________________

____

____

Obj 1.2: ____________________

____

____

Goal 2.0: ____________________

Obj 2.1: ____________________

____

____

Obj 2.2: ____________________

____

____

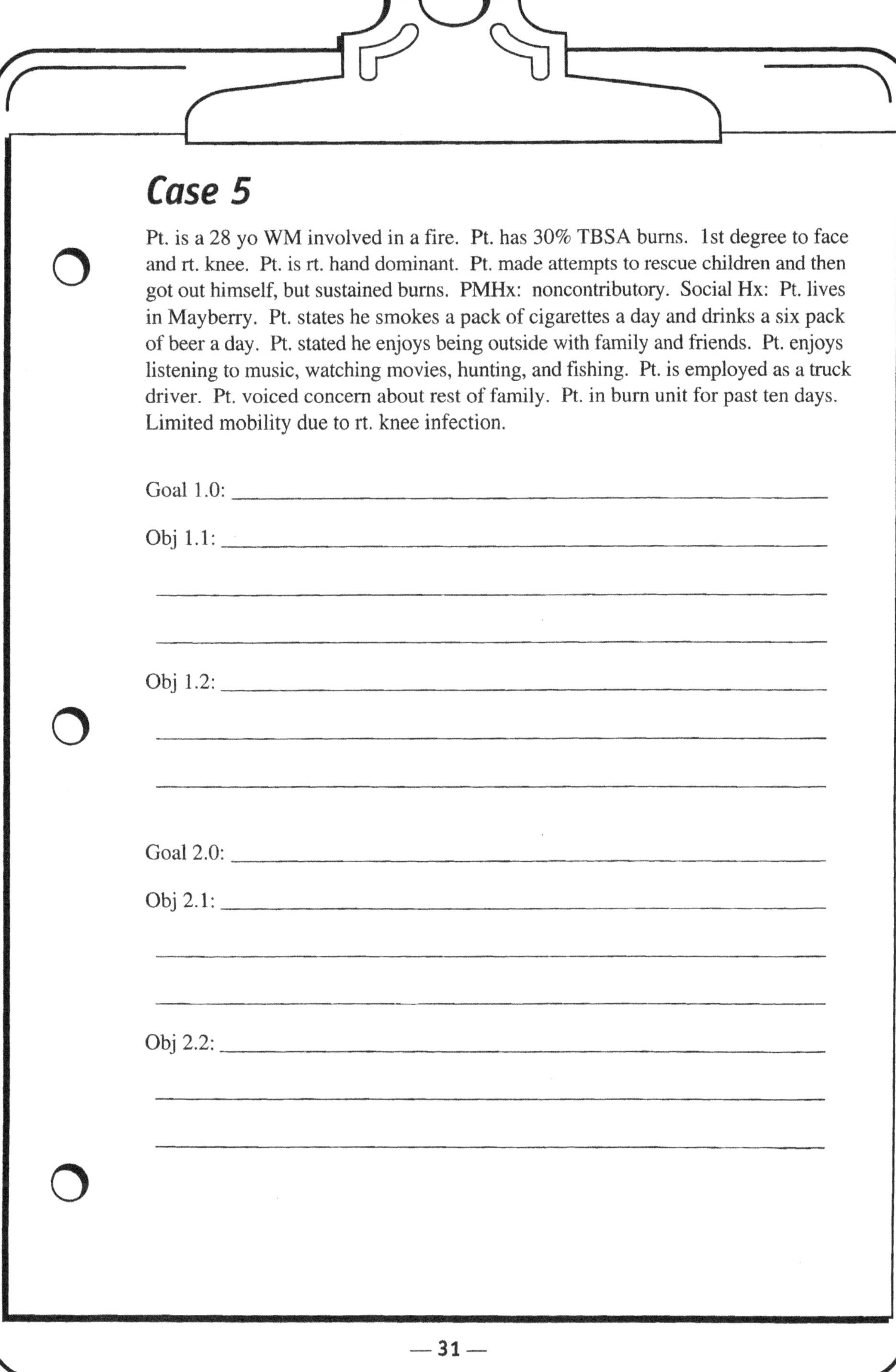

Case 5

Pt. is a 28 yo WM involved in a fire. Pt. has 30% TBSA burns. 1st degree to face and rt. knee. Pt. is rt. hand dominant. Pt. made attempts to rescue children and then got out himself, but sustained burns. PMHx: noncontributory. Social Hx: Pt. lives in Mayberry. Pt. states he smokes a pack of cigarettes a day and drinks a six pack of beer a day. Pt. stated he enjoys being outside with family and friends. Pt. enjoys listening to music, watching movies, hunting, and fishing. Pt. is employed as a truck driver. Pt. voiced concern about rest of family. Pt. in burn unit for past ten days. Limited mobility due to rt. knee infection.

Goal 1.0: ______________________________

Obj 1.1: ______________________________

____

____

Obj 1.2: ______________________________

____

____

Goal 2.0: ______________________________

Obj 2.1: ______________________________

____

____

Obj 2.2: ______________________________

____

____

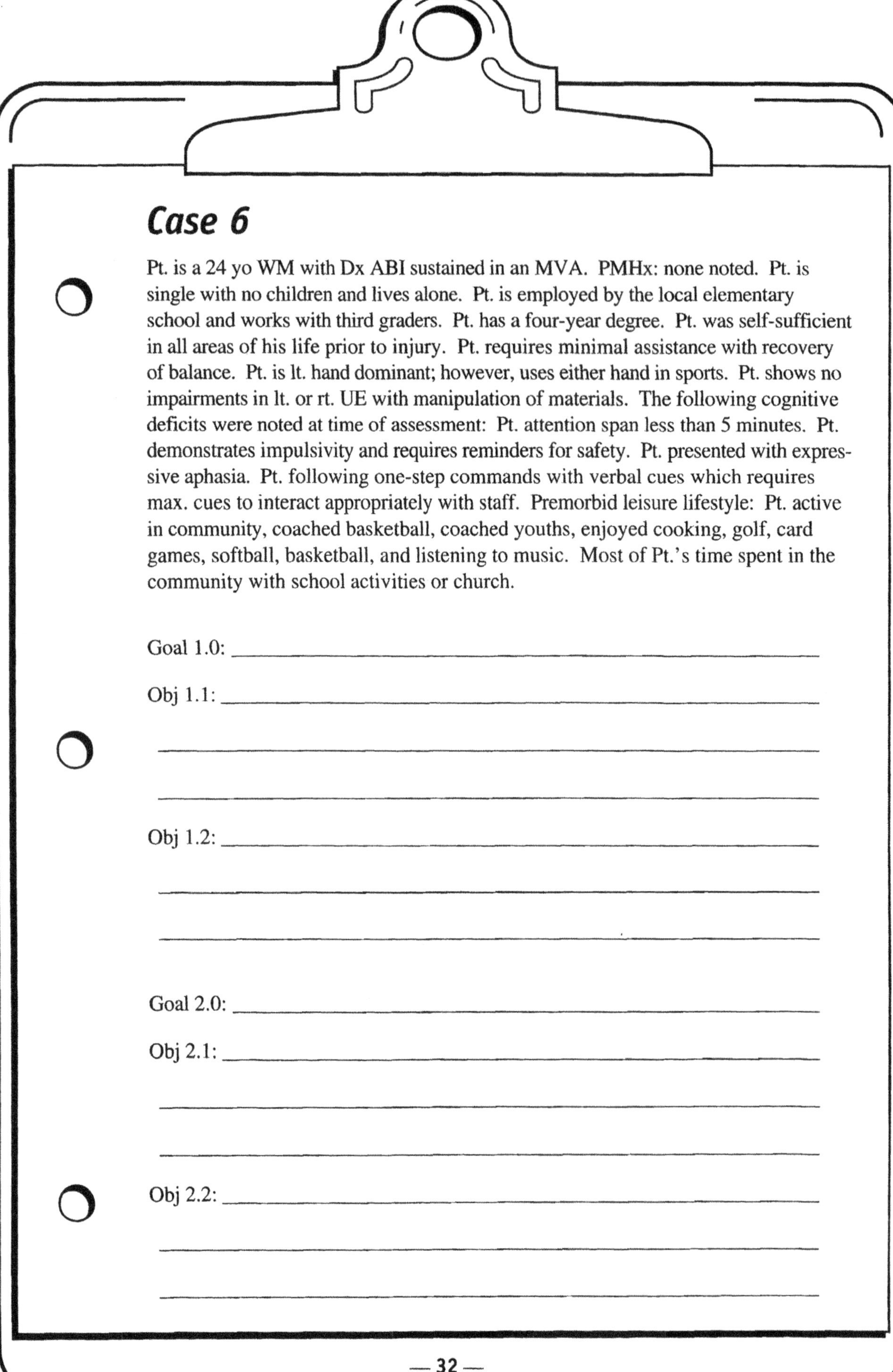

Case 6

Pt. is a 24 yo WM with Dx ABI sustained in an MVA. PMHx: none noted. Pt. is single with no children and lives alone. Pt. is employed by the local elementary school and works with third graders. Pt. has a four-year degree. Pt. was self-sufficient in all areas of his life prior to injury. Pt. requires minimal assistance with recovery of balance. Pt. is lt. hand dominant; however, uses either hand in sports. Pt. shows no impairments in lt. or rt. UE with manipulation of materials. The following cognitive deficits were noted at time of assessment: Pt. attention span less than 5 minutes. Pt. demonstrates impulsivity and requires reminders for safety. Pt. presented with expressive aphasia. Pt. following one-step commands with verbal cues which requires max. cues to interact appropriately with staff. Premorbid leisure lifestyle: Pt. active in community, coached basketball, coached youths, enjoyed cooking, golf, card games, softball, basketball, and listening to music. Most of Pt.'s time spent in the community with school activities or church.

Goal 1.0: ____________________

Obj 1.1: ____________________

____

____

Obj 1.2: ____________________

____

____

Goal 2.0: ____________________

Obj 2.1: ____________________

____

____

Obj 2.2: ____________________

____

____

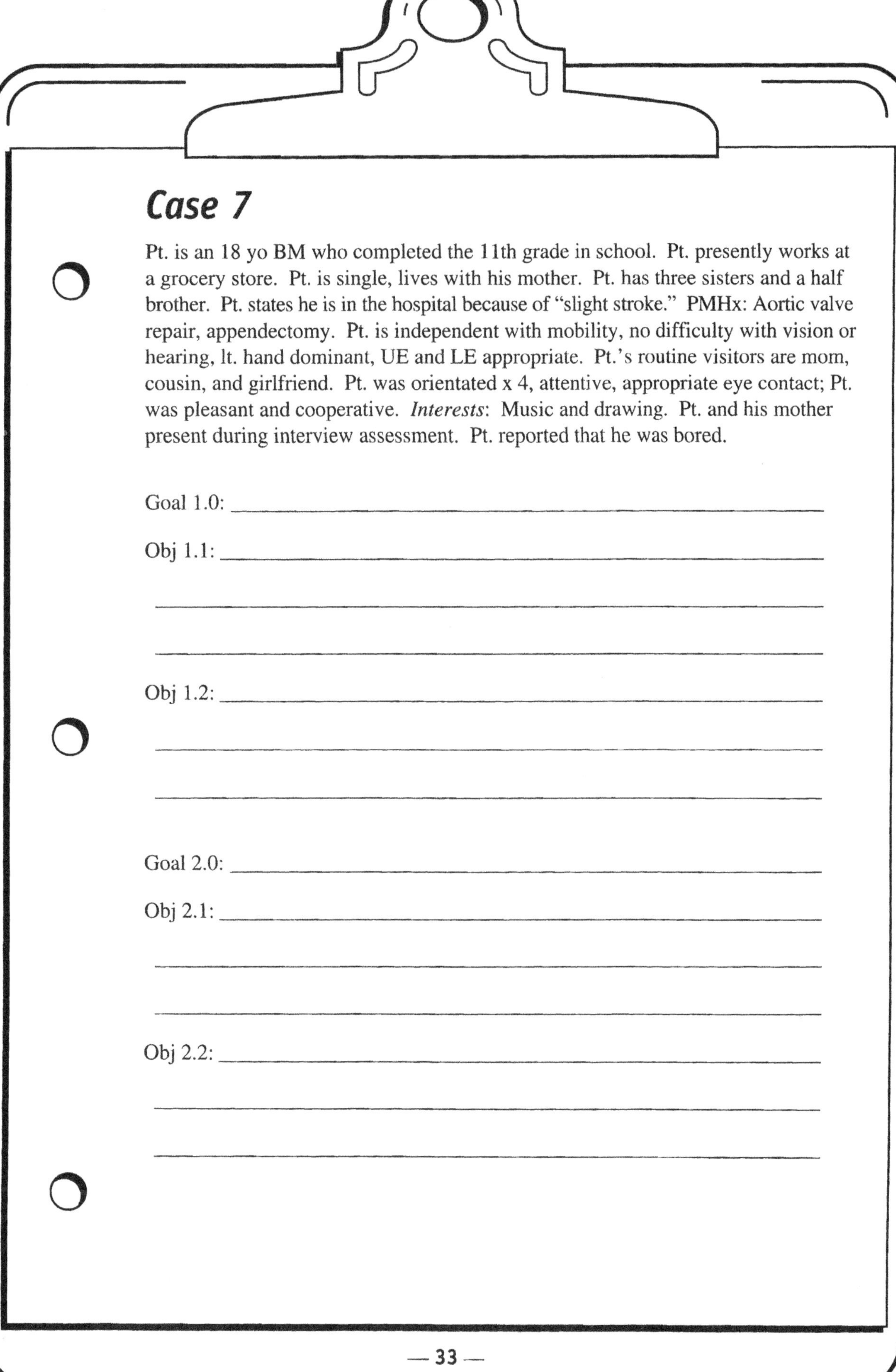

Case 7

Pt. is an 18 yo BM who completed the 11th grade in school. Pt. presently works at a grocery store. Pt. is single, lives with his mother. Pt. has three sisters and a half brother. Pt. states he is in the hospital because of "slight stroke." PMHx: Aortic valve repair, appendectomy. Pt. is independent with mobility, no difficulty with vision or hearing, lt. hand dominant, UE and LE appropriate. Pt.'s routine visitors are mom, cousin, and girlfriend. Pt. was orientated x 4, attentive, appropriate eye contact; Pt. was pleasant and cooperative. *Interests*: Music and drawing. Pt. and his mother present during interview assessment. Pt. reported that he was bored.

Goal 1.0: ______________________________

Obj 1.1: ______________________________

____

____

Obj 1.2: ______________________________

____

____

Goal 2.0: ______________________________

Obj 2.1: ______________________________

____

____

Obj 2.2: ______________________________

____

____

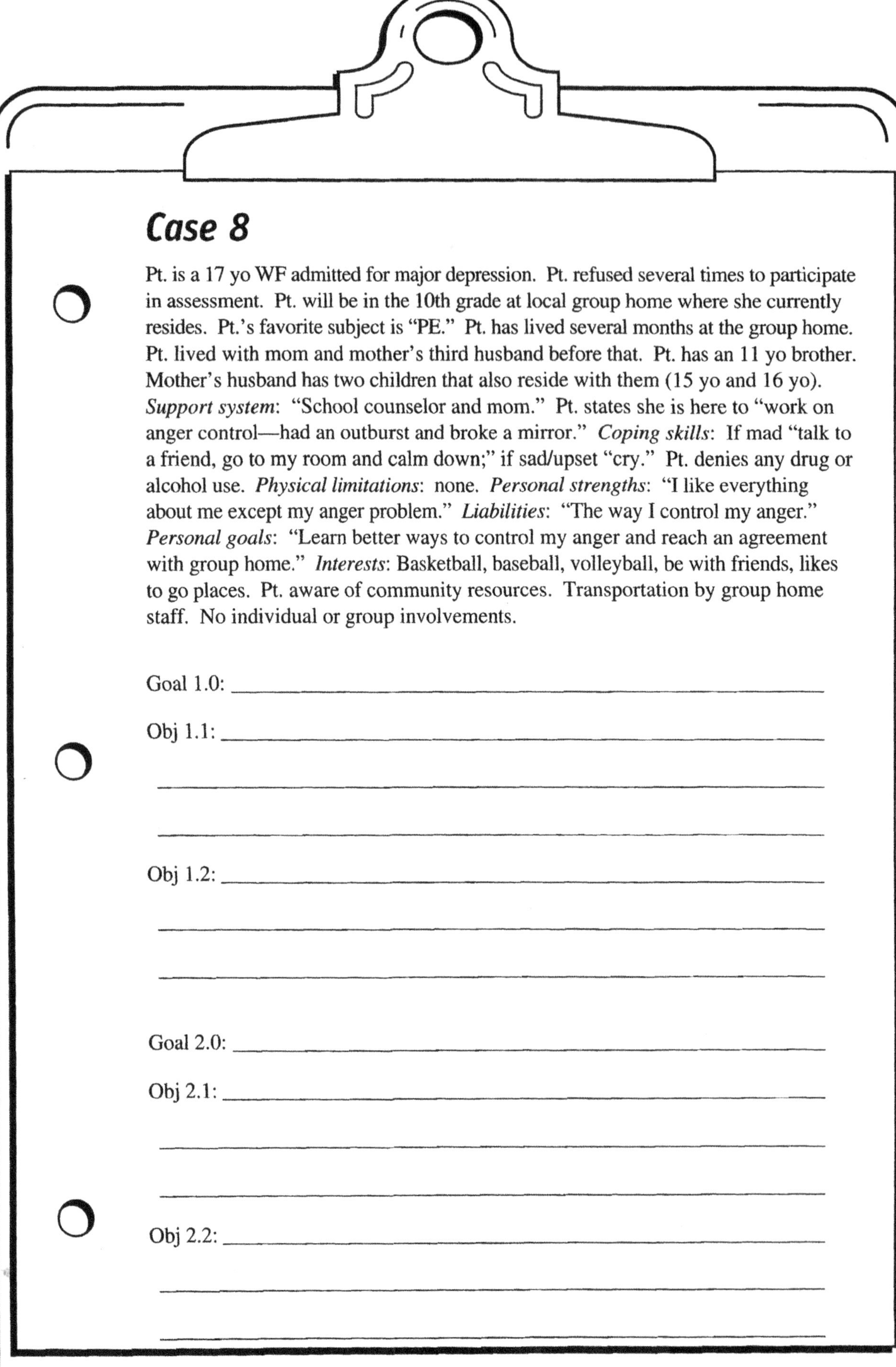

Case 8

Pt. is a 17 yo WF admitted for major depression. Pt. refused several times to participate in assessment. Pt. will be in the 10th grade at local group home where she currently resides. Pt.'s favorite subject is "PE." Pt. has lived several months at the group home. Pt. lived with mom and mother's third husband before that. Pt. has an 11 yo brother. Mother's husband has two children that also reside with them (15 yo and 16 yo). *Support system*: "School counselor and mom." Pt. states she is here to "work on anger control—had an outburst and broke a mirror." *Coping skills*: If mad "talk to a friend, go to my room and calm down;" if sad/upset "cry." Pt. denies any drug or alcohol use. *Physical limitations*: none. *Personal strengths*: "I like everything about me except my anger problem." *Liabilities*: "The way I control my anger." *Personal goals*: "Learn better ways to control my anger and reach an agreement with group home." *Interests*: Basketball, baseball, volleyball, be with friends, likes to go places. Pt. aware of community resources. Transportation by group home staff. No individual or group involvements.

Goal 1.0: ____________________

Obj 1.1: ____________________

____

____

Obj 1.2: ____________________

____

____

Goal 2.0: ____________________

Obj 2.1: ____________________

____

____

Obj 2.2: ____________________

____

____

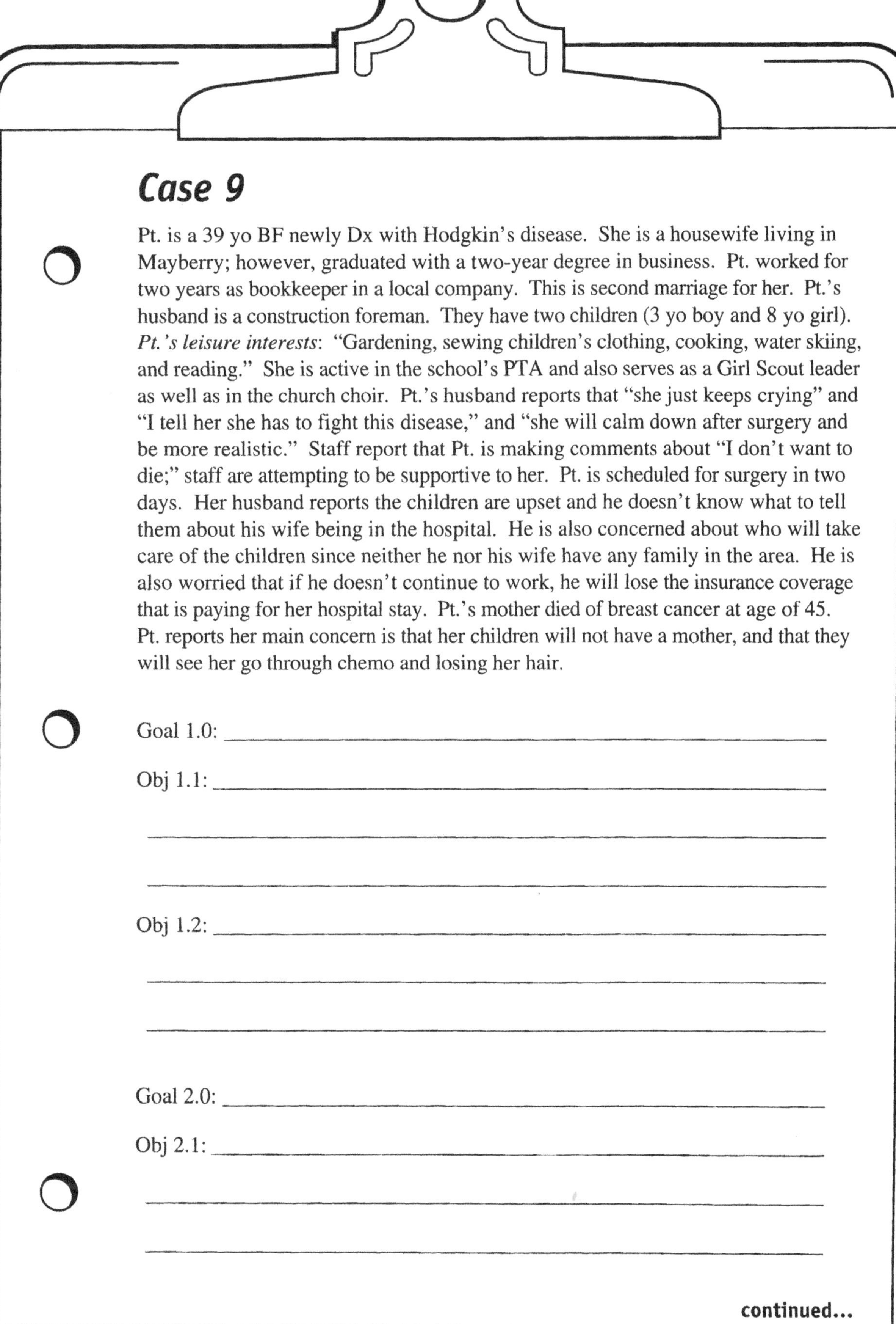

Case 9

Pt. is a 39 yo BF newly Dx with Hodgkin's disease. She is a housewife living in Mayberry; however, graduated with a two-year degree in business. Pt. worked for two years as bookkeeper in a local company. This is second marriage for her. Pt.'s husband is a construction foreman. They have two children (3 yo boy and 8 yo girl). *Pt.'s leisure interests*: "Gardening, sewing children's clothing, cooking, water skiing, and reading." She is active in the school's PTA and also serves as a Girl Scout leader as well as in the church choir. Pt.'s husband reports that "she just keeps crying" and "I tell her she has to fight this disease," and "she will calm down after surgery and be more realistic." Staff report that Pt. is making comments about "I don't want to die;" staff are attempting to be supportive to her. Pt. is scheduled for surgery in two days. Her husband reports the children are upset and he doesn't know what to tell them about his wife being in the hospital. He is also concerned about who will take care of the children since neither he nor his wife have any family in the area. He is also worried that if he doesn't continue to work, he will lose the insurance coverage that is paying for her hospital stay. Pt.'s mother died of breast cancer at age of 45. Pt. reports her main concern is that her children will not have a mother, and that they will see her go through chemo and losing her hair.

Goal 1.0: ____

Obj 1.1: ____

____

____

Obj 1.2: ____

____

____

Goal 2.0: ____

Obj 2.1: ____

____

____

continued...

Obj 2.2: ______________________________

____

____

Case 10

Pt. is a 44 yo HM who was admitted with a spinal cord injury as a result of an MVA and is now a T5 complete paraplegic. Pt. is a traveling salesman for a medical supply company and was traveling to a client's office when he lost control of his car and hit a bridge. There were no other passengers in the car at the time, and the highway patrol charged Pt. with exceeding a safe speed. The car was a total loss. Pt. recalls little about the accident. Pt. is expected to be in the hospital for 3–4 wks. After his time here, it is expected that he will go to an outpatient rehabilitation facility close to his home in Mayberry. Pt. is married and has two children (10 yo and 7 yo sons). His wife has recently quit her teaching job because she is 8 months pregnant and after the birth of the third child was planning on staying at home with the children. Pt. lives a significant distance from the hospital. *Pt.'s Leisure Interests*: "Tennis, yard work, reading, competitive swimmer in high school, and coaching his son's soccer team." Pt. was teary throughout the interview and stated, "What difference does it make about what I used to enjoy?" In a telephone interview with Pt.'s wife she states she is "scared about what changes will have to be made, but if anyone can adapt to the change, it's our family." She states that her husband has "been a wonderful role model for the kids on the soccer team." She admits she is at a loss about how to tell the children that their dad is "paralyzed, and is going to be in a wheelchair for the rest of his life."

Goal 1.0: ____

Obj 1.1: ____

____

____

Obj 1.2: ____

____

____

continued...

Goal 2.0: ___

Obj 2.1: ___

___

___

Obj 2.2: ___

___

___

Possible Goals and Objectives for Case Examples

Following each of the case examples are possible goals and objectives for each of the ten case studies. All of the examples include the three components of a well-written objective (i.e., performance, condition, and criteria).

Case 1

46 yo male, unemployed, receives disability for "chronic nerve condition." Master's in engineering. Hx of ETOH use x 30 yrs, currently denies ETOH is a problem, states it does not "have control" over him. Was involved in AA x 2 mtgs. approx. 10 yrs. ago. Hx of multi-drug abuse (LSD, heroin, cocaine). Smokes marijuana 2–3 x joints/wk. States panic attacks. Gives reason for admission as "depression" and "problems in my marriage." Currently separated from 3rd wife. *Interests*: Watching TV, particularly sports, and visiting the neighborhood bar. *Strengths*: "Intelligence" and "I can talk to anybody." *Liabilities*: "Bad nerves," "marriage." States no support system. Gives typical day as "eating, sleeping, and watching soap operas." Has been in trouble with the law in the past, but would not elaborate.

Goal 1.0: Increase awareness of nonalcohol-related community resources.

Obj 1.1: Pt. will complete leisure inventory worksheet provided by CTRS and mark all the leisure activities that interest him in one 45 min. session.

Obj 1.2: Given a local telephone book, Pt. will form a written list of 5 recreational/leisure sites that interest him by the end of the first 1 hour Leisure Education class.

Goal 2.0: Decrease anxiety.

Obj 2.1: After instruction and demonstration of 3 stress management techniques (tension/release of muscles, deep breathing and meditation, and guided imagery) by therapist, Pt. will repeat preferred relaxation technique autonomously in 1:1 sessions x 2 within a one-week time span.

Obj 2.2: Given worksheets on stress management, Pt. will complete (in writing) and discuss results with CTRS by one week.

Goal 3.0: Increase insight into personal value system.

Obj 3.1: After verbal review of group rules by therapist, Pt. will remain seated within the group circle for the full session (45 min.) regardless of viewpoints verbalized, 1 out of the 2 wkly sessions, for a 2 wk time span.

Obj 3.2: After discussion of situational handouts provided by therapist, Pt. will verbalize a minimum of 1 negative consequence resulting from current value system, per each 1 hour Values Clarification group (held 2 x week) for 2 weeks.

Case 2

70 yo male, Hx of seizures, hearing deficit in rt. ear, c/o arthritis in lt. knee. Resident of Mayberry Family Care Home x 2 yrs. Requires verbal prompting for ADLs. *Interests*: "Dancing, country music, latch hook, watching sports on TV, sleeping." *Strengths*: "Good dancer," "good cook," "keep things clean around the home." *Liabilities*: "I'm fat," "Want to get married."

Goal 1.0: Monitor current level of physical functioning.

Obj 1.1: During a 30-min exercise group, Pt. will duplicate 50% of tasks as instructed by recreation therapist with less than 5 verbal prompts for each session.

Obj 1.2: Given time on the track, Pt. will initiate days he will participate in walking program and walk at least 3x in the first week.

Goal 2.0: Community reintegration.

Obj 2.1: Pt. will verbalize one community resource of interest selected from a list (e.g., YMCA line dancing class, local senior citizen band) provided by CTRS, by the end of one 30 min. leisure education session.

Obj 2.2: Given a daily schedule of 3 groups for the day, Pt. will select one community outing to attend with no more than one prompt by CTRS.

Case 3

16 yo female, currently repeating ninth grade. Lives with biological mother and stepfather, 3 siblings (6 mo, 3 yo, and 5 yo) of this above union. Biological father lives in California, no correspondence x 6 yrs. Patient has a Hx of running away. Currently 3 mo pregnant, wants to keep baby, but boyfriend wants to abort. States reason for admission as attempted suicide by overdose (Tylenol), this reportedly resulted from an argument with boyfriend over pregnancy. States difficulty in saying "no." *Interests*: "TV, walking around the mall." *Strengths*: "Love my baby," "nice." *Liabilities*: "Bad temper" and "I don't have many friends." Patient has isolated herself to her bedroom since admission. Affect flat with depressed mood.

Goal 1.0: Increase insight into personal well-being.

Obj 1.1: Given a personal journal notebook and pen, Pt. will express feelings (write or illustrate) in her journal on a daily basis without prompting for one week.

Obj 1.2: Within three days and without prompting, Pt. will initiate one 1:1 session with CTRS to discuss her feelings of being on the unit.

Goal 2.0: Increase socialization.

Obj 2.1: Upon request, Pt. will introduce herself (state name) 1x in every recreation therapy group attended for one day.

Obj 2.2: Given a structured problem-solving group task, Pt. will initiate conversation without prompting, with at least one peer during each one hour session, 2 out of 5 sessions per week, for her initial week of group involvement.

Goal 3.0: Increase assertion skills.

Obj 3.1: After verbal description by therapist of the three communication styles (passive, aggressive, and assertive behaviors), Pt. will report to the group the behavior that she most often portrays before the end of the first assertiveness class.

Obj 3.2: Within one week and after two assertiveness classes, Pt. will demonstrate by role-play with peer two characteristics of the assertive style of communication.

Case 4

25 yo female, mountain bike competitor and instructor. Obtained injury to L5 region as the result of a fall during a competition 2 mo ago. Pt. is engaged and has temporarily postponed wedding, which was scheduled in 2 wk, stating, "I want to be able to walk down the aisle." *Interests*: "Bike riding, basketball, swimming, shopping, playing with my computer, cross-stitch." *Strengths*: "Well-organized, work well with people, sports, intelligent." *Liabilities*: "Well, I can't walk," "too responsible," "I'm dependent on everybody."

Goal 1.0: Increase awareness of alternative leisure activities.

Obj 1.1: Given a list of leisure videos (highlighting individuals with spinal cord injuries), Pt. will select one video of interest to view and process with therapist. Pt. will complete task within the one hour session.

Obj 1.2: Given a choice of possible activities to complete in general recreation session, Pt. will select one activity and complete in one hour.

Goal 2.0: Demonstrate independent leisure functioning.

Obj 2.1: Given the community resource guide to Mayberry, Pt. will verbally identify three accessible facilitates of interest to therapist by the seventh day of treatment.

Obj 2.2: Given scheduled outing time with CTRS and staff, Pt. will practice her wheelchair mobility skills in the community, at location chosen from Obj 2.1 by two weeks.

Case 5

Pt. is a 28 yo WM involved in a fire. Pt. has 30% TBSA burns. 1st degree to face and rt. knee. Pt. is rt. hand dominant. Pt. made attempts to rescue children and then got out himself, but sustained burns. PMHx: noncontributory. Social Hx: Pt. lives in Mayberry. Pt. states he smokes a pack of cigarettes a day and drinks a six pack of beer a day. Pt. stated he enjoys being outside with family and friends. Pt. enjoys listening to music, watching movies, hunting, and fishing. Pt. is employed as a truck driver. Pt. voiced concern about rest of family. Pt. in burn unit for past ten days. Limited mobility due to rt. knee infection.

Goal 1.0: Increase coping skills by 2 weeks.

Obj 1.1: Given one prompt Pt. will talk about feelings of being in the hospital 3 out of the 4 weekly recreation therapy sessions as deemed successful by therapist by one week.

Obj 1.2: During recreation therapy session, Pt. will practice relaxation therapy techniques as instructed by CTRS for pain management 2x per week.

Obj 1.3: Given relaxation therapy techniques, Pt. will select one technique to engage independently 3x per week and self-report completion to CTRS.

Goal 2.0: Increase leisure functioning.

Obj 2.1: During recreation therapy session, Pt. will explore (and verbalize thoughts of) assistive technology devices while involved in leisure activity of fishing by one week.

Obj 2.2: During recreation therapy session, Pt. will complete paper work to order assistive devices that will assist him in his leisure activity of fishing by two weeks.

Case 6

Pt. is a 24 yo WM with Dx ABI sustained in an MVA. PMHx: none noted. Pt. is single with no children and lives alone. Pt. is employed by the local elementary school and works with third graders. Pt. has a four-year degree. Pt. was self-sufficient in all areas of his life prior to injury. Pt. requires minimal assistance with recovery of balance. Pt. is lt. hand dominant; however, uses either hand in sports. Pt. shows no impairments in lt. or rt. UE with manipulation of materials. The following cognitive deficits were noted at time of assessment: Pt. attention span less than 5 minutes. Pt. demonstrates impulsivity and requires reminders for safety. Pt. presented with expressive aphasia. Pt. following one-step commands with verbal cues which requires max. cues to interact appropriately with staff. Premorbid leisure lifestyle: Pt. active in community, coached basketball, coached youths, enjoyed cooking, golf, card games, softball, basketball, and listening to music. Most of Pt.'s time spent in the community with school activities or church.

Goal 1.0: Increase orientation within 6 wks.

Obj 1.1: Given memory book, Pt. will identify by pointing to his name, place, time, and situation when asked by recreation therapist with no more than 3 verbal cues by 3 weeks.

Obj 1.2: Given memory book and calendar, Pt. will select current month, day, and year with no more than 3 verbal cues x 3 weeks.

Goal 2.0: Increase cognitive functioning within 6 weeks.

Obj 2.1: Given memory book, Pt. will "route" from his room to his first session with recreation therapist with no more than 2 prompts by staff by 4 weeks.

Obj 2.2: During one recreation therapy session, Pt. will complete 1 activity (e.g., puzzle, computer game, peg board) as instructed with no more than 3 cues by 3 weeks.

Case 7

Pt. is an 18 yo BM who completed the 11th grade in school. Pt. presently works at a grocery store. Pt. is single, lives with his mother. Pt. has three sisters and a half brother. Pt. states he is in the hospital because of "slight stroke." PMHx: Aortic valve repair, appendectomy. Pt. is independent with mobility, no difficulty with vision or hearing, lt. hand dominant, UE and LE appropriate. Pt.'s routine visitors are mom, cousin, and girlfriend. Pt. was orientated x 4, attentive, appropriate eye contact; Pt. was pleasant and cooperative. *Interests*: Music and drawing. Pt. and his mother present during interview assessment. Pt. reported that he was bored.

Goal 1.0: Increase leisure awareness by 2 weeks.

Obj 1.1: Given leisure assessment inventories, Pt. will complete and discuss the results with CTRS by the end one 45 min. session.

Obj 1.2: Given instruction on leisure activities in community, Pt. will self report one activity to be involved in prior to discharge and discuss with CTRS by one week.

Goal 2.0: Increase leisure opportunities by 2 weeks.

Obj 2.1: Pt. will select leisure activity to participate in of his choice during recreation therapy session 2x week by one week.

Obj 2.2: During recreation therapy session, Pt. will select three leisure activities of interest to utilize during free time in absence of CTRS and family members by one week.

Case 8

Pt. is a 17 yo WF admitted for major depression. Pt. refused several times to participate in assessment. Pt. will be in the 10th grade at local group home where she currently resides. Pt.'s favorite subject is "PE." Pt. has lived several months at the group home. Pt. lived with mom and mother's third husband before that. Pt. has an 11 yo brother. Mother's husband has two children that also reside with them (15 yo and 16 yo). *Support system*: "School counselor and mom." Pt. states she is here to "work on anger control—had an outburst and broke a mirror." *Coping skills*: If mad "talk to a friend, go to my room and calm down;" if sad/upset "cry." Pt. denies any drug or alcohol use. *Physical limitations*: none. *Personal strengths*: "I like everything about me except my anger problem." *Liabilities*: "The way I control my anger." *Personal goals*: "Learn better ways to control my anger and reach an agreement with group home." *Interests*: Basketball, baseball, volleyball, be with friends, likes to go places. Pt. aware of community resources. Transportation by group home staff. No individual or group involvements.

Goal 1.0: Increase anger control by 2 weeks.

Obj 1.1: Given three classes of anger management, Pt. will verbalize in class three ways to control her anger that are positive by one week.

Obj 1.2: Given anger management worksheets, Pt. will complete all worksheets and discuss with CTRS by one week.

Goal 2.0: Leisure opportunities to practice anger control skills 2 weeks.

Obj 2.1: During leisure group activity (basketball, volleyball, or softball), Pt. will demonstrate anger control skills with no prompts from CTRS by one week.

Obj 2.2: During recreation therapy session, Pt. will discuss three benefits of leisure activities (such as sports) to defuse her anger by one week.

Case 9

Pt. is a 39 yo BF newly Dx with Hodgkin's disease. She is a housewife living in Mayberry; however, graduated with a two-year degree in business. Pt. worked for two years as bookkeeper in a local company. This is second marriage for her. Pt.'s husband is a construction foreman. They have two children (3 yo boy and 8 yo girl). *Pt.'s leisure interests*: "Gardening, sewing children's clothing, cooking, water skiing, and reading." She is active in the school's PTA and also serves as a Girl Scout leader as well as in the church choir. Pt.'s husband reports that "she just keeps crying" and "I tell her she has to fight this disease," and "she will calm down after surgery and be more realistic." Staff report that Pt. is making comments about "I don't want to die;" staff are attempting to be supportive to her. Pt. is scheduled for surgery in two days. Her husband reports the children are upset and he doesn't know what to tell them about his wife being in the hospital. He is also concerned about who will take care of the children since neither he nor his wife have any family in the area. He is also worried that if he doesn't continue to work, he will lose the insurance coverage that is paying for her hospital stay. Pt.'s mother died of breast cancer at age 45. Pt. reports her main concern is that her children will not have a mother, and that they will see her go through chemo and losing her hair.

Goal 1.0: Increase coping skills by 3 weeks.
Obj 1.0: Given 45 min. recreation therapy session prior to Pt.'s surgery, Pt. will be encouraged to vent concerns related to surgery and state current level of coping.
Obj 1.2: Given recreation therapy discussion of relaxation techniques prior to surgery, Pt. will state one relaxation technique to practice by end of session.
Obj 1.3: Given support group on unit, Pt. will attend x 1 session prior to surgery.
Goal 2.0: Family support by 3 weeks.
Obj 2.1: Given recreation therapy session with Pt.'s husband, Pt.'s husband will initiate contact with local Hodgkin's support group for emotional support by one week.
Obj 2.2: Given recreation therapy session for support, Pt. and Pt.'s husband will contact their church to arrange for assistance with the care of their children by one week.

Case 10

Pt. is a 44 yo HM who was admitted with a spinal cord injury as a result of an MVA and is now a T5 complete paraplegic. Pt. is a traveling salesman for a medical supply company and was traveling to a client's office when he lost control of his car and hit a bridge. There were no other passengers in the car at the time, and the highway patrol charged Pt. with exceeding a safe speed. The car was a total loss. Pt. recalls little about the accident. Pt. is expected to be in the hospital for 3–4 wks. After his time here, it is expected that he will go to an outpatient rehabilitation facility close to his home in Mayberry. Pt. is married and has two children (10 yo and 7 yo sons). His wife has recently quit her teaching job because she is 8 months pregnant and after the birth of the third child was planning on staying at home with the children. Pt. lives a significant distance from the hospital. *Pt.'s Leisure Interests*: "Tennis, yard work, reading, competitive swimmer in high school, and coaching his son's soccer team." Pt. was teary throughout the interview and stated, "What difference does it make about what I used to enjoy?" In a telephone interview with Pt.'s wife she states she is "scared about what changes will have to be made, but if anyone can adapt to the change, it's our family." She states that her husband has "been a wonderful role model for the kids on the soccer team." She admits she is at a loss about how to tell the children that their dad is "paralyzed, and is going to be in a wheelchair for the rest of his life."

Goal 1.0: Increase leisure functioning skills utilizing water-based activity by 4 weeks.
Obj 1.1: Given aquatic therapy session, after discussion of safety issues, Pt. will self-report safety issues in reference to pool entry and exit with no more than 2 prompts by 2 weeks.
Obj 1.2: Given life preserver, Pt. will demonstrate proper securing technique of safety equipment with no prompts by 4 weeks.
Goal 2.0: Community reintegration by 4 weeks.
Obj 2.1: Given recreation therapy session, Pt. will discuss his current interest in continuing to coach his child's soccer team and state three issues that need to be addressed in reference to his current level of physical functioning by 2 weeks.
Obj 2.2: Given recreation therapy session, Pt. will plan an outing to soccer field where he coaches to address accessibility issues related to his wheelchair by 4 weeks.

Step into My Office

What is it really like to do an assessment and develop goals and objectives? When a patient is brought to the child/adolescent psychiatry unit, he or she is either voluntarily or involuntarily committed. The majority arrive with the interest of receiving help. The physicians, nurses, psychologist, social workers, and recreation therapist begin their assessment. Typically the recreation therapist's assessment is performed in the activity room or in the recreation therapy office. It is important to provide an environment that is conducive to gathering information or observing the patient's behavior and motor abilities. There are times when the information is gathered while engaging the patient in a game, such as Foosball, while at the same time building a rapport with him or her.

What would you do if you had gathered only bits and pieces for your assessment because the patient was uncooperative? You could excuse the patient after explaining to him or her that you will need to complete the assessment at a later time. Document the patient's current level of uncooperativeness. Then approach the patient at another time (make sure that you give the patient some control to come speak with you and, at the least, you give him or her a date and time to follow up.).

How would you handle a patient that gives "getting out of the hospital" as his or her goal? This is not an uncommon response to, "What would you like to work on while you are here?" or, "What is your goal?" It is up to the therapist at this point to assist the patient in identifying his or her liabilities and to offer ways that recreation therapy can assist him or her in overcoming these problems if he or she so desires. There have been cases were I have offered several ideas and the patient continues to refuse them. At this point I have offered the patient time to think. Usually they are willing to try one goal to address one of their problem areas.

Conclusion

Having completed this manual, it is hoped that you feel more confident in your ability to write goals and objectives that are easy to understand and measurable. As stated earlier, many professionals do not enjoy the process of writing goals and objectives, but realize their value as a means to measure outcomes. Documenting in the patient's chart clear goals and objectives demonstrates to the insurance companies what the patient is actually achieving while involved in treatment with you, the recreation therapist. The ability to write quality goals and objectives may even help in making your services being billable.

It's time to test your basic knowledge of goals and objectives as discussed in this manual. Please complete the post-test on the next page and compare the correct answers with your score from the pretest. If you are interested in additional resources to support the process of writing goals and objectives, consult the following annotated bibliography.

Post-Test

Please answer the following questions after completing manual and compare with pretest.

1. A measurable description of a performance that you want a patient to demonstrate.
   a. Goal
   b. Objective
   c. Criteria
   d. Adjective

2. Important stipulations or limitations under which a performance is expected to occur.
   a. Intent
   b. Performance
   c. Indicator
   d. Condition

3. A performance that can be observed directly (e.g., draw, swim).
   a. Overt
   b. Covert
   c. Visual
   d. Audio

4. Quality or level of performance that will be considered acceptable.
   a. Condition
   b. Criterion
   c. Excellence
   d. Graduated

5. Statements that sound good, but are not very useful.
   a. Pseudo-intellectual stimulation
   b. Wacky
   c. Gibberish
   d. Computer jargon

6. The general direction of intent.
   a. North, South, East, and West
   b. Motivation
   c. Behavior
   d. Goal

continued...

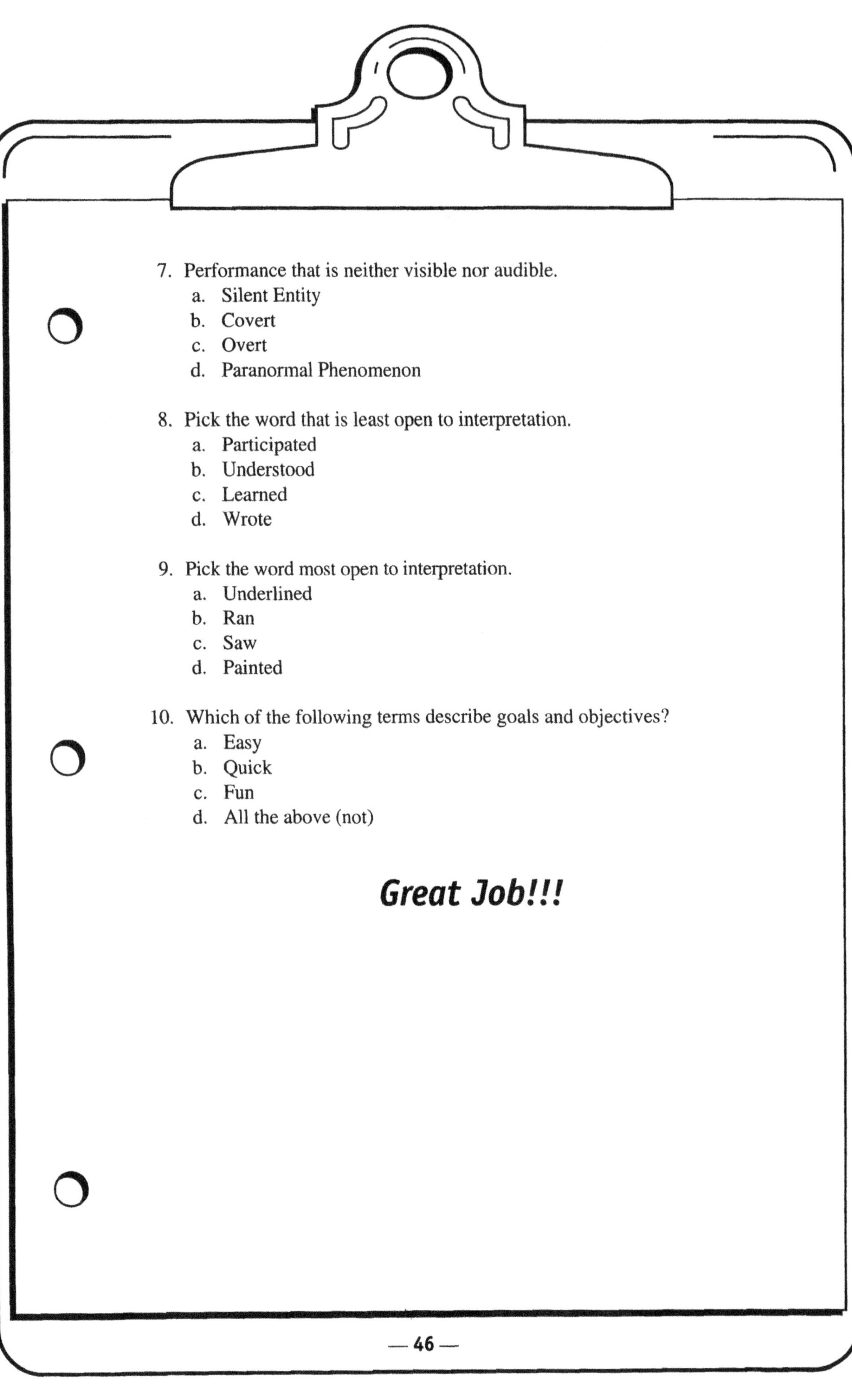

7. Performance that is neither visible nor audible.
   a. Silent Entity
   b. Covert
   c. Overt
   d. Paranormal Phenomenon

8. Pick the word that is least open to interpretation.
   a. Participated
   b. Understood
   c. Learned
   d. Wrote

9. Pick the word most open to interpretation.
   a. Underlined
   b. Ran
   c. Saw
   d. Painted

10. Which of the following terms describe goals and objectives?
    a. Easy
    b. Quick
    c. Fun
    d. All the above (not)

Great Job!!!

Recommended Resources

Adams, J. (1995). *Getting people involved in life and activities: Effective motivating techniques*. State College, PA: Venture Publishing, Inc.

A useful resource for students beginning their internship and/or the new recreation therapist who is just starting out in a psychiatric or long-term care facility. The text reminds recreation therapists that there are many factors that influence a patient's involvement in activities. This directly affects how the recreation therapist will write the necessary goals for and with his or her patients. Recreation therapists are encouraged to recall the importance of control, that is, the need that patients have for a sense of control. An easy way to address this issue is simply to include the patient in the development of his or her goals. Remember, we can break down large goals into simple objectives so that all abilities can achieve success, goal attainment, and/or quality of life. Chapter 4 specifically shows that the therapeutic recreation process consists of four steps: assessment, planning, intervention, and evaluation (i.e., APIE) (p. 17).

Allen, R. and Allen, S. (1997). *Winnie-the-Pooh on success: In which you, Pooh, and friends learn about the most important subject of all*. New York, NY: Dutton.

In chapter three where Pooh and The Stranger are stuck, everyone sets goals, and Alexander Beetle begins to ACHIEVE one, the writers discuss what goals are. As they perceive it "a goal is the result or achievement toward which effort is directed" (p. 45). Although this text is addressing goals as a means to attain personal success, the authors reinforce points that recreation therapists need to remember, such as "One of the things that is bad about having others set goals for you is that you may not be very interested in achieving them or you might not even realize that others have set a goal for you" (p. 47).

Beitz, J. (1996). Developing behavioral objectives for perioperative staff development. *AORN Journal, 64*(1), 87–95.

This article supports the importance of developing clear objectives to create measurability for learning. Beitz states that in teaching the required information (educational needs and process) the nurse educators must break it down—"a first step to bridging this gap is to develop behavioral or learning objectives (i.e., clear statements that describe intended instructional outcomes)" (p. 87). Beitz is specifically speaking to nurse educators; however, the information is helpful to the recreation therapist who must also remember some of the basic theories to learning. As in the field of recreation therapy, nurses have also discussed the time-consuming task of writing objectives. Beitz also states that clear objectives help to motivate the learner to achieve and, provided this occasion, are more likely to be successful. Clear objectives are easier for the individual to work toward and achieve. If the objective is vague, then the individual begins to second-guess what is required to be successful. Beitz reminds the reader of the basics to developing behavioral objectives: "the level of the learner, the necessary components of objectives, and the types and hierarchies of objectives" (p. 88). Discussed is the importance of selecting verbs carefully and specifically to meet what it is you are expecting. Like Mager, Beitz states "the verbs *name* or *recall* can be evaluated objectively;" however, a verb like "*understand* is not concise and can mean anything from recognizing a hemostat to being able to assist with transphenoidal hypophysectomy" (p. 93). The text is a reminder to keep the objective simple and not to list several outcomes such as "identify and analyze" because the individual may be able to do one, but not the other. Simple, concise objectives that are realistic will be easier to attain. It is important to ask questions about what it is that you want the individual to achieve and what is necessary for this process to occur.

Buettner, L. and Martin, S. (1995). *Therapeutic recreation in the nursing home*. State College, PA: Venture Publishing, Inc.

An entire chapter is allocated for Goal Planning (Chapter 3, pp. 31–36). The authors suggest that recreation therapists select no more than three goals to work on at time with the client to avoid confusion of and time constraints on both parties involved. Involvement of the client in his or her goal is encouraged to maximize the client's understanding and motivation. The authors stress the importance of this process by stating "her wishes should be considered above all others" (p. 31).

Charboneau, B. and Murphy, R. (1987). *Therapeutic recreation intervention: An ecological perspective*. Englewood Cliffs, NJ: Prentice Hall, Inc.

What are the implications for the recreation therapist in developing programs for patient's with various disabilities? Chapter 7 discusses variation in disabilities and what modifications the therapist must make, or awarenesses the recreation therapist must have to allow for the individual's full inclusion into activity. Once the recreation therapist has a general understanding of disabilities, it is necessary to remember that these are general and that each individual responds and is affected differently, and also to remember that goals and objectives allow the patient to participate in desired activities. As recreation therapists it is our clinical task to assist the patient in setting realistic goals and objectives. Chapter 10, pages 209–216 are beneficial to read for specific examples of the importance of goals and objectives, their necessary components (time and condition) and evaluation (documentation).

Davidson, J. (1998). *The complete idiot's guide to reaching your goals*. New York, NY: Alpha Books.

This book offers nonthreatening methods to address goal development on a personal level; however, these same skills could be utilized by the professional in groups and individual sessions with patients to develop their goals from a clinical perspective. Chapter 1 covers the basics to goal development. Chapter 4 goes over primary goals and potential steps to reach the goal. The authors provide a "Thought-Diet Card," which is a tool to help the person striving for a goal to stay focused each day on their desired outcome and the methods necessary to achieve the goal. Part 3, Secrets of Master Goal-Setters, shares excellent worksheet opportunities and addresses the importance of proper wording, writing it down on paper, setting a time frame for achievement, and the need to reaccess goals. Jeff Davidson states in Chapter 12, Personalizing Your Goals, "It suffices to say that a goal you identify as being worthy of you and worth the pursuit is no less valid whether it is imposed externally or is the result of another's influence on you" (p. 149). Recreation therapists can assist patients and clients in identifying and developing their goals.

Elliot, A. and Harackiewicz, J. (1994). Goal setting, achievement orientation, and intrinsic motivation a mediational analysis. *Journal of Personality and Social Psychology, 66*(5), 968–979.

This study explores the difference between assigned goals and task-orientated goals and the effects on the intrinsic motivation of the individual. The study came to two conclusions "consideration of the distinction between performance and mastery goals led us to discover that performance goals tend to undermine intrinsic motivation, whereas mastery goals effectively maintain interest" (p. 978). Once again, it is important for us to know our patient's needs and, with the suggestion of this study, what methods work to motivate them. Clear communication with the patient is a must in developing measurable goals and objectives that help to lead toward attainment of long-term goals.

Grote, K., Hasl, M., Krider, R., and Mortensen, D. (1995). *Behavioral health protocols for recreational therapy*. Ravensdale, WA: Idyll Arbor, Inc.

An excellent source to assist recreation therapy students and professionals in the development of goals and objectives. Pages 63–147 explain what to include in the treatment plan and specific examples of goals and objectives. The authors also include terminology that recreation therapy students or professionals can use in their documentation. The terminology is broken into two categories of negative and positive (negative—assaultive, chattering, grumpy; positive—directable, mannerly, friendly). Clear usage of terminology in documentation will make for clearer goals and objectives.

Hinshaw, S. and Melnick, S. (1996). What they want and what they get: The social goals of boys with ADHD and comparison boys. *Journal of Abnormal Child Psychology, 24*(2), 169–185.

This research studied the interaction of ADHD boys in one group versus the comparison boys (non-ADHD or ODD) in the development of their social goals in games of Foosball in a summer camp experience. The boys basically desired similar outcomes from their goals. However the ADHD boys typically went about achieving them in a counterproductive manner that the authors stated is typical of their rejection from their peers. The authors leaned away from the hyperactivity (inattention) as the source for peer rejection, but focused upon the high aggressiveness. "Goals serve as an organizational framework and a guiding rationale for behavior (Wyer and Srull, 1986), and they shape children's behavior and perceptions of the social environment in reciprocal fashion" (p. 180–181). This study demonstrates the need for recreation therapists to program appropriate social goals that can help the ADHD child be more accepted in social settings by addressing the ADHD child's goal and how they perceive their place in social settings. It was interesting to read the author's note about the manner in which the ADHD boys and comparison boys communicated their goals and "a fruitful area of future research may lie in the investigation of the ways goals are communicated through behavior and detected by others" (p. 182).

Kelland, J. (1995). *Protocols for recreation therapy programs*. State College, PA: Venture Publishing, Inc.

This source reinforces the necessity of recreation therapists to be flexible in meeting the desired requirements of their given facility when addressing goals and objectives. The recreation therapy staff at Alberta Hospital, Edmonton did a beautiful job of compiling their programs into protocol forms that address the general program purpose, program descriptions, deficits the program might address, facilitation techniques, staff responsibilities/requirements, expected outcomes, outcome attainment scales, and appendices. I would encourage the recreation therapist to pay close attention to the deficits the program might address, expected program outcomes, and the program outcome attainment scale. The program outcome attainment scales address each client's ability to meet goals (i.e., increase awareness of barriers to leisure involvement) and are evaluated by the client's ability or inability to state or perform in a specific manner.

Program: Leisure Education
Expected Program Outcome—Increase Awareness of Barriers to Leisure Involvement:
0) Unable to recognize any barriers to leisure involvement.
1) Able to recognize that barriers to leisure exist.
2) Able to list personal barriers to leisure involvement.
3) Able to explain the impact personal barriers have had on his/her leisure involvement. (p. 37).

The use of a scale of 0–3 allows measurability. On their forms, there is an area for tracking the client's progress through assessment dates and review dates. It is still the responsibility of the recreation therapist to discuss with the patient what his or her goals are and adjust accordingly. Having prefabricated program goals and objectives will make the task of documentation easier.

King, I. (1996). The theory of goal attainment in research and practice. *Nursing Science Quarterly, 9*(2), 61–66.

It is valuable to our profession to learn what areas other professions are conducting research in that may assist us in our delivery of care to patients and clients. In this article, an overall review of King's Theory for Goals Attainment is addressed. King is a nurse educator who has proposed a theory for increasing quality nursing care to patients through utilization of goals. Her research reveals that nurses share one basic goal for their patients—health. Goals are set with patients by "including the actions of assessing, planning, implementing, and evaluating nursing care" (King, 1996). In the research conducted by Sowell and Lowenstein, "the theory of goal attainment can provide a framework for a variety of health delivery systems that seek to implement and evaluate quality services" (1994, p. 30). Also discussed is the importance of documentation. King discussed "nursing theory based practice provides concrete evidence about the effectiveness of nursing care when mutual goal-setting leads to goal attainment and is documented in the patient's record" (King, p. 64). As in our field of recreation therapy, it is vital to state patient goals and to include the patient/resident in this developmental process. Documentation of the patient's progress is essential.

Mager, R. (1984). *Preparing instructional objectives (2nd ed.).* Belmont, CA: David S. Lake.

This book is 132 pages in length. It is easy to read and understand. It takes the reader through the necessary components to prepare instructional objectives. An excellent companion manual for any recreation therapist's collection.

Manual for recreation therapy in long-term care facilities. (1995). New York, NY: State and National Therapeutic Recreation Society a branch of the National Recreation and Park Association.

This manual is short and concise. It focuses on the important aspects of providing care for individuals in a long-term care facility. Two important steps in this process are writing progress notes and discharge summaries on the client. In each of the steps, the recreation therapist is required to address the goals and objectives of the client and the progress he or she has made. The recreation therapist is also reminded of the importance of updating the goals and objectives as needed (p. 18). The manual provides an example of a progress-note form and includes the goal, scope (cognitive, physical, social, and affective), frequency (how many times a week), and duration (time frame per session) model (p. 26).

Nelson, C. and Payton, O. (1997). The planning process in occupational therapy: Perceptions of adult rehabilitation patients. *American Journal of Occupational Therapy, 51*(7), 576–583.

This article specifically addresses the patient's perception of involvement in the development of his or her goals for treatment. Of importance to the recreation therapist is the conclusion that better communication and involvement is needed with the patient in developing goals. The driving factor to improve the communication of goals between therapist and patient is that "limited healthcare dollars will more likely continue to flow to services that can demonstrate a relationship to patient goals" (p. 583). Of further importance, the authors do a good job stating the requirements by CARF, JCAHO, and A Patient's Bill of Rights and Developmental Disabilities Amendments of 1978 [Public Law 95-602]. These organizations and laws further state the importance/expectation of patient participation in goal development.

Ommundsen, Y. and Roberts, G. (1996). Goal orientation and perceived purposes of training among elite athletes. *Perceptual and Motor Skills, 83*(2), 463–471.

This article attempts to duplicate a previous study. It focuses on "a task-oriented goal perspective… when an individual has an interest in the activity for its own sake and the individual's actions are aimed at achieving mastery, learning, or perfecting a skill" (p. 463). The article addressed motivational factors of athletes and the reasons for involvement in training and the sports they participated in.

Again, the importance of the goal to the individual who is striving to achieve it is invaluable to him or her. Otherwise, the motivation would be lacking, and more than likely, the goal would not be attained.

Peterson, C. and Gunn, S. (1984). *Therapeutic recreation program design: Principles and procedures (2nd ed.)*, pp. 267–323. Englewood Cliffs, NJ: Prentice Hall.

Chapter 5, Developing Specific Programs, and Chapter 10, Assessments, are two chapters that, after reviewing the material, would provide you with knowledge about key components in the therapeutic recreation process. Examples of assessments and how to write goals from a program perspective are offered. Peterson and Gunn are well-known in the field of recreation therapy and this text, like their others, is complete with diagrams (such as p. 294, Figure 10-8 Selection of an Assessment Procedure). It is important to remember that without a thorough and valid assessment of your patient, proper goals and objectives cannot be formulated and achieved.

Reilly, D. (1980). *Behavioral objectives—Evaluation in nursing.* New York, NY: Appleton-Century-Crofts.

"Behavioral objectives, unlike content objectives, are more amenable to evaluation. They are statements that describe the behavior the student is expected to exhibit as a result of one or more learning experiences" (p. 4). "Formulation of these objectives represents the conscious choice of the planners and must be expressed in terms that are clear to all who are involved in implementing them" (p. 26). The authors discuss the need for the behavior objective to be written in a manner that is clear and to the point and directed at the performance of the learner. The objective must be "observable and measurable" (p. 31). "We do not see a person analyze a poem; we see or hear a report of his analysis" (Kibler, Barker, and Miles, 1970, p. 20). The authors remind individuals who are writing behavioral objectives to keep them concise, ask for only one behavior at a time. Although this source was written to develop behavioral objectives for nursing students it is a wonderful comparison source to back up what Mager and others state on the how to's for writing solid objectives.

Strecher, V., Gerard, H., Kok, G., Latham, G., Glasgow, R., DeVellis, B., Meertens, R., and Bugler, D. (1995). Goal setting as a strategy for health behavior change. *Health Education Quarterly, 22*(3), 190–200.

This article discusses goal setting and the attempt to prove whether it is beneficial. It also outlines the characteristic to its success or failure. This article stated the need for continued research. The authors were working under the premise that "goal setting theory predicts that, under certain conditions, setting specific difficult goals leads to higher performance when compared with no goals or vague, nonquantitative goals, such as "do your best"" (p. 190). The authors used the Lee, Locke, and Latham definition for a goal: "...that which one wants to accomplish; it concerns a valued, future end state." Characteristics for developing a goal were explored, and a brief discussion on who is setting the goal was included. In writing goals and objectives, include the following characteristics: motivation, commitment, understanding, and simplicity, while allowing for individual effort from the patient. The therapist can break down complex goals to smaller steps that are easier for the person to achieve. Be sure to address rewards and provide feedback to the patient. It was determined that "a consistent theme emerging from our discussion of goal setting strategies has been the many positive outcomes that may be accrued through effective carefully constructed goal setting procedures" (p. 198).

Tzetzis, G., Kioumourtzoglou, E., and Mavromatis, G. (1997). Goal setting and feedback for the development of instructional strategies. *Perceptual and Motor Skills, 84*(3), 1411–1427.

"In an athletic or instructional setting goal setting (Locke, 1968) has been identified as a useful and valid tool of enhancing performance (Miner, 1984). A considerable amount of research on goal setting has indicated that the use of goals can enhance performance" (Cevrone, Jiwani, and Wood, 1991; Early and Lituchy, 1991; Hall, Weinberg and Jackson, 1987). This article explored the effectiveness of adding feedback with goal-setting. The study showed that goal-setting with feedback provided better outcomes then just the one versus the other. Once again it was noted that "try to do your best" (Locke and Latham (1985) is too vague and does not have the motivating factors to achievement as specific goals.

The article focused on goal setting and feedback both in performance and in results. In the development of goals, the participant was involved in, participated in, and agreed to the goals in the form of a contract. The focus of this article was to determine in the research if learning objectives (basketball-related) were better learned in one fashion over another (KR vs KP vs GS).

References

Adams, J. (1995). *Getting people involved in life and activities: Effective motivating techniques.* State College, PA: Venture Publishing, Inc.

Allen, R. and Allen, S. (1997). *Winnie-the-Pooh on success: In which you, Pooh, and friends learn about the most important subject of all.* New York, NY: Dutton.

Austin, D. and Crawford, M. (1991). *Therapeutic recreation an introduction.* Englewood Cliffs, NJ: Prentice Hall.

Beitz, J. (1996). Developing behavioral objectives for perioperative staff development. *AORN Journal, 64*(1), 87–95.

Buettner, L. and Martin, S. (1995). *Therapeutic recreation in the nursing home.* State College, PA: Venture Publishing, Inc.

Charboneau, B. and Murphy, R. (1987). Intervention: An interaction approach. In (Ed.), *Therapeutic recreation intervention: An ecological perspective.* Englewood Cliffs, NJ: Prentice-Hall, Inc.

Davidson, J. (1998). *The complete idiot's guide to reaching your goals.* New York, NY: Alpha Books.

Elliot, A. and Harackiewicz, J. (1994). Goal setting, achievement orientation, and intrinsic motivation a mediational analysis. *Journal of Personality and Social Psychology, 66*(5), 968–979.

Fuhrer, M. (1997). *Assessing medical rehabilitation practices: The promise of outcomes research.* Baltimore, MD: Paul H. Brookes Publishing Co.

Grote, K., Hasl, M., Krider, R., and Mortensen, D. (1995). *Behavioral health protocols for recreational therapy.* Ravensdale, WA: Idyll Arbor.

Hinshaw, S. and Melnick, S. (1996). What they want and what they get: The social goals of boys with ADHD and comparison boys. *Journal of Abnormal Child Psychology, 24*(2), 169–185.

Kelland, J. (1995). *Protocols for recreation therapy programs.* State College, PA: Venture Publishing, Inc.

Kibler, R., Barker, L., and Miles, D. (1970). *Behavioral objectives and instruction.* Boston, MA: Allyn Bacon, p. 20.

King, I. (1996). The theory of goal attainment in research and practice. *Nursing Science Quarterly, 9*(2), 61–66.

Mager, R. (1984). *Preparing instructional objectives (2nd ed.).* Belmont, CA: David S. Lake.

Manual for recreation therapy in long-term care facilities. (1995). New York, NY: State and the National Therapeutic Recreation Society, a branch of the National Recreation and Park Association.

Nelson, C. and Payton, O. (1997). The planning process in occupational therapy: Perceptions of adult rehabilitation patients. *American Journal of Occupational Therapy, 51*(7), 576–583.

Ommundsen, Y. and Roberts, G. (1996). Goal orientation and perceived purposes of training among elite athletes. *Perceptual and Motor Skills, 83*(2), 463–471.

Peterson, C. and Gunn, S. (1984). Assessment. In *Therapeutic recreation program design: Principles and procedures (2nd ed.),* pp. 267–323. Englewood Cliffs, NJ: Prentice Hall.

Reilly, D. (1980). *Behavioral objectives—Evaluation in nursing.* New York, NY: Appleton-Century-Crofts.

Strecher, V., Gerard, H., Kok, G., Latham, G., Glasgow, R., DeVellis, B., Meertens, R., and Bugler, D. (1995). Goal setting as a strategy for health behavior change. *Health Education Quarterly, 22*(3), 190–200.

Tzetzis, G., Kioumourtzoglou, E., and Mavromatis, G. (1997). Goal setting and feedback for the development of instructional strategies. *Perceptual and Motor Skills, 84*(3), 1411–1427.

Appendix: Charting and Prescription Abbreviations

Complied from *Taber's Cyclopedic Medical Dictionary, 17th ed.* (1993). Philadelphia, PA: F.A. Davis Co.

Abbreviation	Latin Phrase (unless noted)	English Definition
$\overline{aa}$ or a	ana (Greek)	of each
abs. feb.	absente febre	without fever
a.c.	ante cibum	before eating
add.	adde	add
ad effect.	ad effectum	until effectual
adhib.	adhibendus	to be administered
admov.	admove	apply
ad part. dolent.	ad partes dolentes	to the painful parts
ad sat.	ad saturatum	to saturation
adst. feb.	adstante febre	when fever is present
ad us.	ad usum	according to custom
ad us. ext.	ad usum externum	for external use
aeq.	aequales	equal
ag. feb.	aggrediente febre	when the fever increases
agit.	agita	shake, stir
agit. ante sum.	agita ante sumendum	shake before taking
alb.	albus	white
alt. dieb.	alternis diebus	every other day
alt. hor.	alternis horis	every other hour
alt. noc.	alternis nocte	every other night
alter	alter	the other
aq.	aqua	water
aq. bull.	aqua bulliens	boiling water
aq. cal.	aqua calida	warm water
aq. dest.	aqua destillata	distilled water
aq. ferv.	aqua fervens	hot water
aq. font.	aqua fontis	spring water
aq. frig.	aqua frigida	cold water
aq. menth. pip.	aqua menthae piperitae	peppermint water
aq. pur.	aqua pura	pure water
aut	aut	or
bal.	balneum	bath
bal. sin.	balneum sinapis	mustard bath
bene	bene	well
bib.	bibe	drink
b.i.d.	bis in die	twice a day
b.i.n.	bis in noctus	twice a night
bis	bis	twice
bis in 7d.	bis in septem diebus	twice a week
BP		blood pressure
bol.	bolus	a large pill
bull.	bulliat	let (it) boil
$\bar{c}$	cum	with
cap.	capsula	a caspsule
cat.	cataplasma	a poultice
chart., cht.	chartula	a small medicated paper
cito disp.	cito dispensetur	let it be dispensed quickly
c.m.	cras mane	tomorrow morning
c.m.s.	cras mane sumendus	to be taken tomorrow morning
c.n.	cras nocte	tomorrow night
coch. mag.	cochleare magnum	a tablespoonful
coch. med.	cochleare medium	a dessertspoonful
coch. parv.	cochleare parvum	a teaspoonful
collyr.	collyrium	an eyewash
commisce	commisce	mix together
comp.	compositus	compounded of

Abbreviation	Latin Phrase (unless noted)	English Definition
cont. rem.	continuetur remedia	let the medicine be continued
cotula	cotula	a measure
cuj. lib.	cujus libet	of any you please
c.v.	cras vespere	tomorrow night
cyath.	cyathus	glassful
cyath. vinos.	cyathus vinosus	wineglassful
D	dosis	dose
d.	da	give
d	dies	day
/d		daily
d.d. in d.	de die in diem	from day to day
dec.	decanta	pour off
decub.	decubitus	lying down
dent. tal. dos.	dentur tales doses	give of such doses
det	detur	let be given
dieb. alt.	diebus alternis	every other day
dieb. tert.	diebus tertiis	every third day
dil.	dilue, dilutus	dilute, diluted
dim.	dimidius	one-half
div.	divide	divide
div. in p. aeq.	dividatur in partes aequales	let it be divided into equal parts
donec alv. sol. ft.	donec alvus soluta fuerit	until bowels are open
dos.	dosis	dose
dur. dolor.	durante dolore	while pain lasts
e.m.p.	ex modo prescripto	as directed
emp.	emplastrum	plaster
emuls.	emulsio	an emulsion
en., enem.		enema
epistom.	epistomium	a stopper
exhib.	exhibeatur	let it be given
ext.	extende	spread
	extractum	extract
ferv.	fervens	boiling
f.h.	fiat haustus	let a draught be made
filt.	filtra	filter
f.m.	fiat mistura	let a mixture be made
f.p.	fiat potio	let a potion be made
f. pil.	fiat pilula	let a pill be made
ft.	fiat	let it be made
garg.	gargarisma	a gargle
grad.	gradatim	by degrees
gtt.	gutta, guttae	a drop, drops
guttat.	guttatim	by drops
haust.	haustus	a draught
h.n.	hoc nocte	tonight
hor. decub.	hora decubitus	bedtime
hor. som., h.s.	hora somni	at bedtime
hor. 1 spat.	horae unius spatio	one hour's time
idem	idem	the same
in d.	in dies	daily
inf.	infusum	let it infuse
int.	intime	thoroughly
lin.	linimentum	a liniment
liq.	liquor	a solution
lot.	lotio	a lotion
M.	misce	mix
mac.	macera	macerate
man. prim.	mane primo	first thing in the morning
mas.	massa	mass
med.	medicamentum	a medicine
m. et n.	mane et nocte	morning and night

Abbreviation	Latin Phrase (unless noted)	English Definition
mist.	mistura	mixture
mitt.	mitte	send
mitt. x tal.	mitte decem tales	send ten like this
mod.	modicus	moderate sized
mod. praesc.	modo praescripto	as prescribed
moll.	mollis	soft
mor. dict.	more dicto	in the manner directed
mor. sol.	more solito	in the usual manner; as accustomed
n.b.	note bene	note well
ne tr. s. num.	ne tradas sine numo	deliver not without the money
no.	numero	number
noct.	nocte	night
noct. maneq.	nocte maneque	night and morning
non. rep., n.r.	non repetatur	let it not be repeated
noxt.	noxte	night
nunc	nunc	now
omn. bid.	omnibus bidendis	every two days
omn. bih.	omni bihoris	every second hour
omn. hor.	omni hora	every hour
omn. noct.	omni nocte	every night
omn. ¼ h.	omni quadrantae horae	every fifteen minutes
om. mane vel. noc.	omni mane vel nocte	every morning or night
p.a.a.	parti affectae applicetur	let it be applied to the affected region
part. aeq.	partes aequales	equal parts
part. vic.	partitus vicibus	individual doses
pil.	pilula	a pill
p.o.	per os	by mouth
post. cib., p.c.	post cibum	after meals
p.p.a.	phiala prius agitata	the bottle being shaken first
p.r.	per rectum	through the rectum
p.r.n.	pro re nata	as needed
pro. rat. aet.	pro ratione aetatis	according to patient's age
pulv.	pulvis	powder
p.v.	per vaginam	through the vagina
red. in pulv.	redactus in pulverem	reduced to powder
repetat., rep.	repetatur	to be repeated
rub.	ruber	red
Q.h.	quaque hora	every hour
Q.2h.		every two hours
Q.3h.		every three hours
q.i.d.	quater in die	four times a day
q.l.	quantum libet	as much as is wanted
q.p.	quantum placeat	at will
q.s.	quantum sufficiat	a sufficient quantity; as much as may be needed
quotid.	quotidie	daily
s.a., sec.a.	secundum artem	by skill
semih.	semihora	half an hour
sig.	signa	write
	signetur	let it be labeled
sing.	singulorum	of each
sol.	solutio	solution
solv.	solve	dissolve
s.o.s.	si opus sit	if necessary
ss.	semi or semisse	a half
st.	stet (stetem)	let it (them) stand
subind.	subinde	frequently
sum.	sume	take
	sumat, sumendum	let him take, to be taken
sum. tal.	sumat talem	take 1 such
suppos.	suppositoria	a suppository
s.v.	spiritus vini	alcoholic spirit

Abbreviation	Latin Phrase (unless noted)	English Definition
s.v.r.	spiritus vini rectificatus	rectified spirit of wine
s.v.v.	spritus vini vitis	brandy
T.		temperature
tab.	tabella	a tablet
tere	tere	rub
tere bene	tere bene	rub well
t.i.d.	ter in die	three times daily
t.i.n.	ter in nocte	three times a night
tinct.	tinctura	a tincture
trit.	tritura	triturate or grind
ult. praes.	ultimus praescriptus	the last ordered
ung.	unguentum	an ointment
ur		urine
ut. dict.	ut dictum	as directed
vitel.	vitellus	yolk of an egg

The A•B•Cs of Behavior Change: Skills for Working With Behavior Problems in Nursing Homes
by Margaret D. Cohn, Michael A. Smyer and Ann L. Horgas

Activity Experiences and Programming Within Long-Term Care
by Ted Tedrick and Elaine R. Green

The Activity Gourmet
by Peggy Powers

Advanced Concepts for Geriatric Nursing Assistants
by Carolyn A. McDonald

Adventure Education
edited by John C. Miles and Simon Priest

Aerobics of the Mind: Keeping the Mind Active in Aging—A New Perspective on Programming for Older Adults
by Marge Engelman

Assessment: The Cornerstone of Activity Programs
by Ruth Perschbacher

Behavior Modification in Therapeutic Recreation: An Introductory Manual
by John Datillo and William D. Murphy

Benefits of Leisure
edited by B. L. Driver, Perry J. Brown and George L. Peterson

Benefits of Recreation Research Update
by Judy M. Sefton and W. Kerry Mummery

Beyond Bingo: Innovative Programs for the New Senior
by Sal Arrigo, Jr., Ann Lewis and Hank Mattimore

Beyond Bingo 2: More Innovative Programs for the New Senior
by Sal Arrigo, Jr.

Both Gains and Gaps: Feminist Perspectives on Women's Leisure
by Karla Henderson, M. Deborah Bialeschki, Susan M. Shaw and Valeria J. Freysinger

Dimensions of Choice: A Qualitative Approach to Recreation, Parks, and Leisure Research
by Karla A. Henderson

Effective Management in Therapeutic Recreation Service
by Gerald S. O'Morrow and Marcia Jean Carter

Evaluating Leisure Services: Making Enlightened Decisions
by Karla A. Henderson with M. Deborah Bialeschki

Everything From A to Y: The Zest Is up to You! Older Adult Activities for Every Day of the Year
by Nancy R. Cheshire and Martha L. Kenney

The Evolution of Leisure: Historical and Philosophical Perspectives, Second Printing
by Thomas Goodale and Geoffrey Godbey

Experience Marketing: Strategies for the New Millennium
by Ellen L. O'Sullivan and Kathy J. Spangler

File o' Fun: A Recreation Planner for Games & Activities—Third Edition
by Jane Harris Ericson and Diane Ruth Albright

The Game Finder—A Leader's Guide to Great Activities
by Annette C. Moore

Getting People Involved in Life and Activities: Effective Motivating Techniques
by Jeanne Adams

Great Special Events and Activities
by Annie Morton, Angie Prosser and Sue Spangler

Inclusive Leisure Services: Responding to the Rights of People With Disabilities
by John Dattilo

Internships in Recreation and Leisure Services: A Practical Guide for Students, 2nd Edition
by Edward E. Seagle, Jr., Ralph W. Smith and Lola M. Dalton

Interpretation of Cultural and Natural Resources
by Douglas M. Knudson, Ted T. Cable and Larry Beck

Intervention Activities for At-Risk Youth
by Norma J. Stumbo

Introduction to Leisure Services—7th Edition
by H. Douglas Sessoms and Karla A. Henderson

Leadership and Administration of Outdoor Pursuits, Second Edition
by Phyllis Ford and James Blanchard

Leadership in Leisure Services: Making a Difference
by Debra J. Jordan

Leisure and Leisure Services in the 21st Century
by Geoffrey Godbey

The Leisure Diagnostic Battery: Users Manual and Sample Forms
by Peter A. Witt and Gary Ellis

Leisure Education: A Manual of Activities and Resources
by Norma J. Stumbo and Steven R. Thompson

Leisure Education II: More Activities and Resources
by Norma J. Stumbo

Leisure Education III: More Goal-Oriented Activities
by Norma J. Stumbo

Leisure Education IV: Activities for Individuals With Substance Addictions
by Norma J. Stumbo

Leisure Education Program Planning: A Systematic Approach, Second Edition
by John Dattilo

Other Books by Venture Publishing, Inc.

Leisure in Your Life: An Exploration, Fifth Edition
by Geoffrey Godbey

Leisure Services in Canada: An Introduction
by Mark S. Searle and Russell E. Brayley

Leisure Studies: Prospects for the Twenty-First Century
edited by Edgar L. Jackson and Thomas L. Burton

The Lifestory Re-Play Circle: A Manual of Activities and Techniques
by Rosilyn Wilder

Marketing for Parks, Recreation, and Leisure
by Ellen L. O'Sullivan

Models of Change in Municipal Parks and Recreation: A Book of Innovative Case Studies
edited by Mark E. Havitz

More Than a Game: A New Focus on Senior Activity Services
by Brenda Corbett

Nature and the Human Spirit: Toward an Expanded Land Management Ethic
edited by B. L. Driver, Daniel Dustin, Tony Baltic, Gary Elsner, and George Peterson

Outdoor Recreation Management: Theory and Application, Third Edition
by Alan Jubenville and Ben Twight

Planning Parks for People, Second Edition
by John Hultsman, Richard L. Cottrell and Wendy Z. Hultsman

The Process of Recreation Programming Theory and Technique, Third Edition
by Patricia Farrell and Herberta M. Lundegren

Programming for Parks, Recreation, and Leisure Services: A Servant Leadership Approach
by Donald G. DeGraaf, Debra J. Jordan and Kathy H. DeGraaf

Protocols for Recreation Therapy Programs
edited by Jill Kelland, along with the Recreation Therapy Staff at Alberta Hospital Edmonton

Quality Management: Applications for Therapeutic Recreation
edited by Bob Riley

A Recovery Workbook: The Road Back From Substance Abuse
by April K. Neal and Michael J. Taleff

Recreation and Leisure: Issues in an Era of Change, Third Edition
edited by Thomas Goodale and Peter A. Witt

Recreation Economic Decisions: Comparing Benefits and Costs (Second Edition)
by John B. Loomis and Richard G. Walsh

Recreation for Older Adults: Individual and Group Activities
by Jerold E. Elliott and Judith A. Sorg-Elliott

Recreation Programming and Activities for Older Adults
by Jerold E. Elliott and Judith A. Sorg-Elliott

Recreation Programs That Work for At-Risk Youth: The Challenge of Shaping the Future
by Peter A. Witt and John L. Crompton

Reference Manual for Writing Rehabilitation Therapy Treatment Plans
by Penny Hogberg and Mary Johnson

Research in Therapeutic Recreation: Concepts and Methods
edited by Marjorie J. Malkin and Christine Z. Howe

Simple Expressions: Creative and Therapeutic Arts for the Elderly in Long-Term Care Facilities
by Vicki Parsons

A Social History of Leisure Since 1600
by Gary Cross

A Social Psychology of Leisure
by Roger C. Mannell and Douglas A. Kleiber

Steps to Successful Programming: A Student Handbook to Accompany Programming for Parks, Recreation, and Leisure Services
by Donald G. DeGraaf, Debra J. Jordan and Kathy H. DeGraaf

Therapeutic Activity Intervention With the Elderly: Foundations & Practices
by Barbara A. Hawkins, Marti E. May and Nancy Brattain Rogers

Therapeutic Recreation: Cases and Exercises
by Barbara C. Wilhite and M. Jean Keller

Therapeutic Recreation in the Nursing Home
by Linda Buettner and Shelley L. Martin

Therapeutic Recreation Protocol for Treatment of Substance Addictions
by Rozanne W. Faulkner

A Training Manual for Americans With Disabilities Act Compliance in Parks and Recreation Settings
by Carol Stensrud

Venture Publishing, Inc.
1999 Cato Avenue
State College, PA 16801
Phone: (814) 234-4561; Fax: (814) 234-1651